Overcoming all Odds

My Story of
Adversity,
Tragedy,
Persistence,
Survival
and
Triumph

Carol Ann Wilson

Overcoming all Odds
My Story of Adversity, Tragedy, Persistence, Survival and Triumph
© 2023 Carol Ann Wilson.

All rights reserved.
This book or any portion thereof may not be reproduced or used in any manner whatsoever without the express written permission of the publisher except for the use of brief quotations in a book review.

Proofreader: Peggie Ireland
Cover and Interior Design: Rebecca Finkel, F + P Graphic Design, FPGD.com
Book Publishing Expert: Judith Briles, TheBookShepherd.com

Books may be purchased in quantity by contacting the publisher through the author's website: www.carolannwilson.com

Library of Congress Control Number: 2022920716
ISBN trade paper KDP: 979-8-9870888-0-7
ISBN trade paper Ingram Spark: 979-8-9870888-1-4
ISBN eBook: 979-8-9870888-2-1
ISBN audiobook: 979-8-9870888-3-8

Memoir | Overcoming Adversity | Health | Entrepreneur

First Edition
Printed in the USA

I dedicate this book to my children—
Cheryl Brecko, Scott Wilson, and Marie Flores.

Contents

Author's Note vii
1 In the Beginning 1
2 The Parenting Factor 13
3 My College Years 19
4 Wedding and Honeymoon 29
5 School and Babies 35
6 New Beginning and New Trials 41
7 The Big Move 55
8 My Ostomy Story 59
9 Pottery 73
10 Life Goes On 81
11 A Message from Beyond 89
12 The Next Step 93
13 Psychic Healing 97
14 Back to Work … My New Calling 107
15 A Quantum Leap Is Ahead 117
16 Love Walks In 129
17 Storm Clouds Ahead 141
18 The Tiger Cruise 153
19 Machu Picchu 161
20 Recovering 169
21 Hello World … Here We Come 183
22 My Final Thoughts 191
About Carol Ann Wilson 194
How to Contact Carol Ann 195
Acknowledgments 196

Author's Note …

Like many, I've made it a habit to have my annual checkup early in the year. This year was no different. After turning in the required paperwork, I chatted with one of the assistants. When she found out that I was 85 years old, she was aghast. "What is your secret?" she asked.

My secret?

I thought about that after I left and realized that I had heard this question for many years from a variety of people. What is your secret, Carol Ann?

I have faced incredible challenges that include life-threatening chronic illnesses; surviving cancer; having my business stolen from me—not once, but twice; and having several books that I authored plagiarized and stolen from me. I had to deal with the sudden and totally unexpected death of my husband who was at home while I was cruising in the middle of the Pacific Ocean. And there is much more. Yet none of these happenings kept me down.

Now I posed a few questions to myself:

Could my life's story be a story that touched others because it resonated with their own life experiences … or of those they knew and were close to?

Have my adversities—running the gamut from health to business—enhanced me and what I do instead of knocking me down?

Are there things I've learned in my nine decades that could help others?

This I know: Those who experience difficulties and trauma need to understand that good things can come.

Here is my story.

—*Carol Ann*

1
In the Beginning

Much of my learning about the world
comes from what is between the covers of books.

It was a cold winter day in the heart of South Dakota that I chose to be born. My parents, Gladys and Ray Fraley, were elated with the birth of their first child. That would be me.

The year was 1937 and most women called themselves housewives. Dad was an engineer for the Milwaukee Railroad as an investigator for all things involving train wrecks.

His employment created a childhood of packing up and unpacking. We moved every six months as the train tracks expanded across South Dakota and our family followed them. Eventually Montana came into view and he transitioned to the Montana Highway System. Dad's employment created pain for me when I entered school.

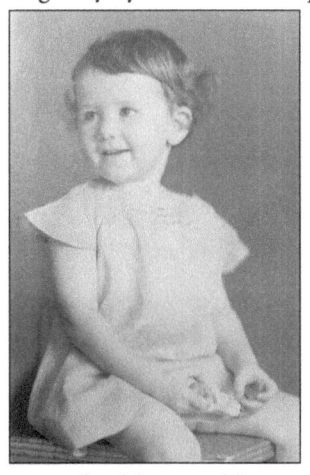

Carol Ann, aged 2

Why? Because every six months meant another move. The constant moving left me stranded. I had no friends. There was nothing permanent about where we were or how long we would be there. Arriving in Butte, Montana, I was five and ready for school but there was no kindergarten. My only option was first grade.

Tall for my age, physically I would fit in with the six year olds. Plus, I could read and was ahead of most kids in the class. From then on, I would always be the youngest in the class and usually the tallest girl.

For the next three years, I was in and out of schools. It was the "every six months" routine when the highway took us to a different part of the state. As I entered each new classroom, it was common for me to keep my head down and pretend no one saw me. Invisible me was usually the last to be picked for anything by my classmates. It hurt.

> To this day, I still read nonstop.

When I was seven, Dad brought me a surprise. It was my first "chapter" book for juveniles: *Five Little Peppers and How They Grew*. My reading appetite came to life. *Heidi* quickly followed. My goal became to read every book in the school library, rarely putting one down until the last page was read. Finally, Mom stepped in. We agreed that I could read as much as I wanted, as long as I would put the book down when she needed me.

To this day, I still read nonstop: more than 100 books a year. Much of my learning about the world comes from what is between the covers of books.

Once again, I was walking into a new classroom, the sixth one in four years. This one was for fourth grade. I thought, "If I keep my head down, they will not notice me." But, of course, they did. I was very shy and would hardly talk to anyone. It was so painful!

Minnesota was our next stop. And we stayed in the same place for three years! It was heaven for me: friends. I had a best friend at last. It was also a place where I experienced mean kids, and some of their antics overshadowed much of my life for years.

Daily, I read the funnies in our local paper. This was the time that B.O. Plenty and Gravel Gertie were common features in the *Dick Tracy* comic strip. B.O. stood for "body odor" and nobody liked to stand close to B.O. Plenty!

When I was in the fifth grade, I was friends with a girl. But one day, that girl became angry with me because I wouldn't give her a stuffed rabbit we had found on the way home from school. For whatever reason, she began telling all our classmates that I had B.O. We would be standing in line and she would say loudly, "Don't stand close to Carol; she has B.O.!" I would be speechless in my pain and misery and my face would get hot with shame. The kids would move away from me.

> **It made me feel ugly and unacceptable.**

After this had happened for three or four days in a row, I ran home from school in tears and tried to explain how awful it was to Mom. She really had no understanding of the terrible pain I was in and tried to make me feel better, but it didn't work. I was ostracized by the others and I'm sure they didn't even know why except that it was a game that had to be kept up. What was incredible was that this went on for the rest of that school year.

The first days of my sixth grade school year were greeted with some trepidation. I was hoping beyond hope that over the summer the kids would have forgotten this awful game and their chanting at me. I remember standing next to Dale at the back of the school room while the teacher was explaining an art project, When one of the kids shouted out, "Dale, watch out! Look who you're standing next to. It's B.O.!"

Dale looked at me, turned to the other boy and said, "So?" And he continued to stand next to me! I was absolutely stunned!

He was my hero. However, the mean name game continued during my sixth grade year but with much less fervor. This bullying made me feel ugly and unacceptable and created emotional scars that took me years and years to overcome.

Their cruelty was transferred to one of our unsuspecting teachers, Miss Olsen. As she would move up and down the aisles to check our work, someone would touch her dress at her butt, and then quickly touch someone else and say, "You have teacher's stink!" And they would pass it around the room without getting caught, giggling or making crude remarks. As I think back about this, I am amazed at the meanness and thoughtlessness of those kids. And sadly, I know that these things happen everywhere.

> **There was a good side: I missed a month of school and no mean kids.**

Around fifth or sixth grade, I became quite ill with whooping cough and pneumonia combined. It was my first time in a hospital and they didn't have enough regular size beds in the children's wing. The only option was to sleep in a crib. Already the tallest in my class in school, my body barely fit. One day, a man passed by my room and stopped. The next thing I heard was laughter … his laughter directed at me for how I looked in that crib. It was bad enough being the tallest, gangly kid in my class, but now a stranger was laughing at me because the hospital didn't have enough beds!

There was a good side: I missed a month of school and no mean kids. So, for a short time, I did not have to endure the cruelty.

During those couple of years, my body was growing incredibly fast. I was well on my way to my final height of five feet ten inches. My legs would constantly ache at night. Sometimes I would cry out in pain at night and Mom would come rub them until the pain went away. She had me checked by doctors but all they ever said was that it was *growing pains*. When I became a mother and was wakened from a sound sleep, I now understood what it had been like for my mom getting up night after night with me.

> **I was mortified and lusted after the penny loafers that my friends had.**

My feet were a problem. The foot doctor said oxfords with lots of support were needed. So ugly oxfords were purchased and became my daily wear. I was mortified and lusted after the penny loafers that my friends had. When it came time for new shoes after the first pair was outgrown, a promise was made to Mom, "I will never run over my heels again." After much pleading, she took a chance and gave in. The coveted penny loafers were now mine. Every single second those shoes were on my feet, walking straight and keeping my heels in place became my goal. I was determined never to have to wear those ugly oxfords again. And with effort on my part, I succeeded.

The highlight of living in Minneapolis was being within a mile of Minnehaha Park. What a treasure that was to ride my bike and spend the whole day in the ravines and forests of the park. Sometimes I would follow the creek down to the Mississippi River to watch the boats and play along the water. It was the only thing that made my mother nervous when I ventured out, but I promised not to go to the river alone. Much of the huge park was unimproved and provided an incredible playground for a young girl who had just read *The Last of the Mohicans* and many Zane Gray books. I became lost in my fantasies of sneaking through the woods and the dirt paths through the forest "rescuing" the prisoners in the primitive park. Things are certainly different now. Today, those paths are concrete with fences alongside. And I don't know of any huge park today where a 12-year-old girl would be safe by herself.

Blue Skies starring Bing Crosby and Joan Caulfield was a movie that all of us had just seen. I was so excited when Mom ran across a small piece in the newspaper that said Joan Caulfield was scheduled to arrive at the Minneapolis airport the next day. With my bicycle, I could pedal out and be there to greet her. Mom gave me an index card for her autograph and I headed out. Those were the days of small terminals where anyone could walk out to the tarmac to greet the plane's passengers when it landed.

The greeters now included me along with a small group of others waiting for the plane, including the mayor. The plane landed, the door opened, and she walked down the stairway. A jeep drove up with the mayor ready to greet her. After everyone else had welcomed her, I decided it was my turn. I walked to the jeep where she was now sitting and asked for her autograph. She very graciously signed my index card. Then the mayor asked, "Don't you want my autograph, too?"

No, I didn't … not on my special card anyway. But I begrudgingly handed him the card and he signed it. I was so disappointed and went home crying to my mother and shouted, "He ruined it! He ruined it!" Years later, I came across that card in my memory box and found that the mayor's name had been Hubert H. Humphrey!

For years, Mom braided my hair every single day in French braids. My hair was long, almost to my waist, and it took her a long time to braid it but she did it every single morning before school. No one at that time seemed to know how to do French braids. Strangers would often comment on them and Mom would teach anyone who asked, using me as the guinea pig! Finally, when I was 12, the braids were gone. I'm not sure whose idea it was to cut them, but I loved it. I felt like a different person! Although anyone with French braids, freckles, and five inches taller than any of the boys couldn't be pretty, I *almost* felt pretty.

My Grandma Fraley was special to me. My father, the only one who went to college, was one of her favorites of her seven children. Maybe that was why I was also a favorite of hers. She gave me books to read and always encouraged me. And she talked to me like an adult. I was only twelve when she died. I had a strong feeling that she was watching me from heaven because, of course, that was where she was. Her death really impacted me and caused me to act in a way to make her proud of me. What a heavy conscience for a young girl to have! But that feeling lasted for years and to this day, I feel her protectiveness around me.

I had started seventh grade in Minneapolis when Dad was told that he would be transferred again. This time it was to be Chicago. As a family, we went to look it over. Mom and Dad couldn't think of any place more awful, so Dad made a big decision. He quit the railroad and headed west to Rapid City, South Dakota, where he teamed up with an old classmate from the South Dakota School of Mines, Damon Matter, and they started their own firm: Matter and Fraley Engineers.

The Matters had four daughters. One was destined to be one of my closest friends. Diane was within a week of my age and we became inseparable immediately. We spent weekends and summers together. This inseparableness lasted until we each were married. After that, no matter how many miles apart we lived, we continued to see each other once or twice a year.

One summer, Diane went with us to visit our relatives in Nebraska. For the first time, I looked at my farm relatives in a different way. I looked at them as I imagined they must have looked to my friend: different. All of a sudden, my down to earth, robust, rollicking, fun cousins seemed rather hickish.

To this day, I still feel ashamed of those feelings. After all, if I didn't have those cousins, I wouldn't have wonderful memories of jumping from the loft in the barn into a haystack; of swinging on a rope out over 20 feet of space and landing in a haymow; of throwing bushels of tomatoes at the walls in the attic—we sure caught hell for that!; of catching fireflies by the jarful; of watching milk being separated and butter being churned; of watching an aunt heat an iron on the wood stove to iron clothes; of sitting around at night by kerosene lantern and playing cards; of church socials with hand-churned ice cream; of feeding chickens and gathering eggs; of watching my aunt wring the chicken's neck that we were having for dinner—something that left me in shock the first time; and dozens of other memories.

From the earliest I can remember, we traveled every summer. And trying to keep three kids in the backseat quiet was a challenge. We used to play games most of the time. Dad would put a nickel on the dash and challenge the rest of us to guess how far a certain spot was down the road; what year and model the next car was that we met; word games, riddles, mind teasers. There wasn't a game that I didn't love. And my greatest triumph was when I could get the answer faster than Dad and win that nickel! These games really stretched my mind. And the family competitions also contributed to my competitive nature!

Now a seventh grader in Rapid City, I learned about the Girl Scouts. I immediately joined a troop led by Elsie Orr whose nickname was Eeyore, like the donkey character in *Winnie the Pooh*. Mom became assistant leader and I started into a world where I excelled, earning as many badges as I possibly could and constantly went for higher and higher honors. New friends came from this arena. At school, I did well with my schoolwork but was never part of the "in" group. The inferiority complex cultivated in my early grade school years was painful and a shadow. Diane, even though we were the same age, was a grade below me so we never did school things together.

> **I owe a lot to the training I had in Scouting.**

Girl Scouting became my arena. In the summertime, I would go to Girl Scout Camp Pahasapa. Although many of my friends would drop out year after year, I would continue. I became an assistant counselor, then a counselor, then a troop leader, then, after 22 years, I was a trainer.

One of the things that was taught and reinforced flowed through our camping experiences during high school. For a primitive camping trip for eight to ten girls required the following: plan the menus; prepare the shopping list; buy the food within the allowed budget; plan the equipment needed for a three-day outing; pack everything; hike to the camping spot; dig latrines; lash tables; prepare campfire site for cooking and evening campfires that was environmentally safe; put up tents; cook meals; cleanup, keep food cold and/or dry and away from animals; and plan activities for everyone like day hikes, games, campfire programs. Then at the end of the camping trip, take down the campsite and leave it looking as though we had not been there.

For a high school girl to accomplish all of this took a lot of knowledge and responsibility. I believed in Scouting and it became a way of life for me. This carried forward into future life. I owe a lot to the training I had in Scouting. When I look back on it now, I see that it was one area that truly did prepare me and became part of my core values for life.

In reality, I was a tomboy. When I was in junior high, I would play tackle football with the boys in the neighborhood. I was the only girl. I was strong and could hold my own. One time, I even bested one of the boys in a wrestling match. He was mortified and never liked me after that. One summer, my father said no more football or wrestling with the boys because I was becoming a young woman.

You have to understand that my parents back then never displayed much emotion. They displayed five times more emotion in their eighties than they did in their forties. And Mom always tried to get the point across to me that it was wrong to be vain or egotistical.

In ninth grade, I decided to have a birthday party. I wanted a new dress that would look smashing and found a picture of a model wearing just the dress I wanted. Mom made all of my clothes, and I knew she could make me look just like that model! We shopped for the pattern and material. When Mom finished sewing the dress and I tried it on, the magic of my mind made me totally beautiful. I asked her, "Am I pretty?"

"You look very nice."

But I pressed her and asked again, "But am I pretty?"

Her response was the same. "You look very nice." Somehow her noncommitment underscored my belief that I was *not* pretty.

It is impossible to talk about my high school days without mentioning one of my teachers, Miss Krieger. She taught all the math classes and I took all of them. She was surely a character and she was a force in molding the character of students who came in touch with her. She wouldn't put up with laziness or answering a question without standing up. I can still hear her saying in her distinctively shrill voice, "Stand up, stand up! You can think better on your feet. After all, the electrons in the air come down from the ceiling, go through your body and down through the floor to help you give the right answer!" And you know, it did seem to help. After she retired from teaching, she continued to tutor the students at the School of Mines where my father had gone years before. She worked with students into her 90s!

An article in the *Reader's Digest* caught Dad's eye about foreign students at Macalester College in St. Paul, Minnesota, being part of a motorcade that toured the western United States. Dad contacted the college and offered to be a host to the motorcade when it came to the Black Hills. Well, that grew and grew. For years, we met and fell in love with students from all over the world. It enriched our lives.

In January of my senior year, the family went on a vacation to California. A secondary reason for the trip was to look over colleges so that I could decide on one to apply to. One stop was Boulder, Colorado. Coming over the hill to Boulder and seeing the red-roofed buildings of the campus created an emotion in me that was like coming home. I knew that was where I was going to school, period. And except for six years during my marriage when we left Boulder, I have lived in the Boulder area since 1954.

2
The Parenting Factor

I learned how important it is to be honest, have integrity and be dependable.

In looking back at events that really shaped my life and why I am the way I am, I have to talk about my parents. With all the magazines and books screaming about dysfunctional families today, child abuse and sexual abuse, I wonder how I escaped all of that.

I spent a lot of time trying to figure out where we were on the scale of wealth. Now I realize that we were average. Dad earned enough so that we could always have what we needed but no more. And from my parents, I learned that while we had everything we needed, we were indeed fortunate—extremely fortunate.

> **From Dad, I learned the strength to always do and be my best.**

For entertainment, we played lots of games. I learned nearly every card game and board game that there was. We also put together lots of jigsaw puzzles. We traveled a lot and we had company. And I always felt free to have friends over.

I took it for granted that Mom and Dad kissed each other every morning before he went out the

Mom and Dad

door and every night when he came back home. In my memory, they never missed a single time. I thought that was just the way life was.

From Dad I learned the strength to always do and be my best. I learned honesty. I learned that I could become whatever I wanted to become. The fact that I was a girl had nothing to do with it. Dad was a "jack of all trades" and I loved watching him work at fixing things around the house. I learned a lot from him. I learned to be efficient. When the book *Cheaper by the Dozen* came out, the father in the book was an efficiency expert and Dad got quite a kick out of that. Dad was a study in efficient motions. When my brother Dick worked for him one summer as rod man while they were surveying, it drove him crazy when Dad would show him how to take the transit out of its case with two movements and no wasted motion. I loved the challenge of finding the least number of steps to do something, especially repetitive motions. I put this knowledge to good use hundreds of times later in life.

> From Mom, I absorbed all the qualities necessary to be proper in any company—even royalty.

I learned that to be trusted was an essential quality. I always swelled with pride when I learned that Dad would be offered a surveying job before others because "Fraley could be trusted to get the job done, do it right, and not overcharge."

These are the things I learned from my dad:

- How to sharpen a knife
- How to make a plumb bob
- How to skin a pheasant
- How to letter (I learned to letter on his architectural drawings well enough that he would actually use me!)

- Friendly bets are fun
- Everyone deserves a Mulligan
- Don't be a quitter
- How to find studs in a wall
- "Hard work never hurt nobody"
- Spend your money wisely and invest your money well
- I can accomplish anything I want
- Be honest, ethical, and trustworthy
- God is there when we ask Him

From Mom, I absorbed all the qualities necessary to be proper in any company—even royalty. I wonder now where she learned all that. Her sayings are priceless:

"Don't eat in front of other people if they have nothing to eat."

"If you can't say something nice, don't say anything at all."

"You should always keep your promise even if you don't want to, so be careful what you promise."

"Always be cheerful. It may lift others' gloomy moods."

"Nothing is that big of a deal."

"We always have enough."

"There are always others worse off than we are."

"If someone is mean or doesn't play fair, don't play with him or her."

"Love your family no matter what."

"Be a lady and act like a lady."

"If your body is getting out of shape, do something about it."

"Pass things around the table. Don't just take something and set the plate down."

"Never talk dirty—or ugly."

"Keep your negative opinions to yourself."

"Never say things in anger that you wouldn't really want to come true."

"Don't show amorous affection in public."

"You don't have to buy the most expensive things to look nice."

"Crowds have a mind of their own. They are not always right and they often turn into a mob and get everyone into trouble, so leave when the crowd starts forming."

Dad paid me a dollar for every time I read Dale Carnegie's *How to Win Friends and Influence People*. That was pretty easy money for me then but Dad knew what he was doing. These lessons were solid and stuck with me. He was generous with his money even though he watched it carefully. When someone was in need, he helped out as best he could, although I usually didn't know about it at the time. And I suspect he tithed all his life to his church.

Mom was the peacemaker. I never knew her to gossip. She would always discourage malicious gossip in our household. She'd say that we didn't know how things looked from the other person's point of view. Maybe the person had had a bad day. She helped me to look at things from someone else's side.

I was always praised for my good grades and good work as long as I did my best. I would be chastised if I did just enough work to get by. It didn't matter what grade I got if I had truly done my best.

When I try to think about how I felt about my parents as a child, I'm having trouble identifying feelings. It's like I spent my childhood being an impassionate observer. I observed my role models to find out how to live life. ***I learned how important it is to be honest, have integrity and be dependable.***

3
My College Years

Eyes exchanged, yet nothing was said.
Then I noticed them peering at a column in the lobby.

The campus of the University of Colorado was hypnotic to me, pulling me in. I loved it. My first living space was Farrand Hall where many became friends. The campus was so crowded that four of us shared a large room to start. One of my roommates was Marianne, someone who was not into being friends. What she was into were pranks. I remember waking up out of a deep sleep to find my hand stuck in a glass of water. She had heard that if you put a sleeping person's hand into warm water, it would make them pee. It didn't.

My education in life was starting! In all the late night discussions with my girlfriends in the dorm, life was not all that I thought it was. I never heard so many heartbreaking stories of dysfunctional families. At first, I didn't believe them. I thought they were making it all up. When I told them my stories, they accused me of making up a *Leave It to Beaver* family. They thought I was the one who was lying! Looking back, I really counted my blessings, even with all the moves I had experienced.

Keep going!
Keep going!

There was a mixer my second evening and I went to it feeling excitement to be in this new environment. Held in the ballroom of University Memorial Center, booths surrounded the perimeter with information about the campus, events, and activities, more like an orientation. Smack in the center was a dancing floor and it wasn't long before the bunny hop started. Of course, I joined the long line right away.

We were all in synch, laughing and having a good time, when suddenly, the people in front of me started slowing down. I pushed the guy in front of me saying, "Keep going! Keep going!" He turned around and looked at me like "Who the heck is this?" By this time, the bunny hop was finished, and he turned again. This time, we formally met. He was Hal Wilson. Hal told me that his friend, Chuck Angevine, was at one of the booths. Curious, I wanted to meet him so we walked over. "How do you know Hal?" I asked Chuck.

Instantly, a loud, raucous, high-pitched laughter erupted from him. "Hal?! Hal?!" And then facing Hal, he said, "Wilson, are you stringing along this lovely girl already?"

> My friends started calling me "the 7-Up Kid."

It turned out that *Hal* never told girls his real name at first in case things didn't work out. Little did he know that he was looking at his future wife! His real name was Lynn Wilson, which caused confusion at times. In fact, the university assigned him to the girls' dorm I was in when he first got on campus!

Classes started and studying occupied most of my time. I dated several other boys during my freshman year, while Lynn and I talked a lot on the phone and met often for coffee or to study. So many of our social activities included going to the Sink or Tulagi's to drink, the go-to beer hangout for us students. My beverage of choice was a 7-Up. My friends started calling me "the 7-Up Kid."

Lynn was wanting to see more and more of me and started sounding serious. I didn't know how I really felt about Lynn and wasn't ready to give up this freedom of meeting different fellows. Finally, I asked him to back off and give me space.

Then a funny thing happened. Some of my friends set me up with a blind date. When I went down to the lounge to meet my friends and their friend that they were excited for me to meet, I asked, "So, where is your friend?" Eyes exchanged, yet nothing was said. Then I noticed them peering at a column in the lobby. From around the back came Lynn, looking very sheepish. I realized it was a setup and saw the humor in it. Laughing warmly, I noticed his face. He was afraid. As he crossed the lobby, his eyes maintaining contact with mine, he said, "I thought you would be angry."

But how could I be? Pretty soon we were all laughing. All of us went out and we had a good time.

During the spring of my freshman year, my application to be an exchange Girl Scout had been accepted. My destination would be Canada for six weeks that summer. It was an incredible honor to be selected along with my travel mates, Bonnie Jean Klees and Patty Jo Divers.

Girl Scout travel mates, Patty Jo Divers and Bonnie Jean Klees

The Canadian Experience

Traveling was a unique experience. First, the only thing I could take was a backpack, so all my clothes and anything else were in it. The setup for it started in New York where the three of us got the lowdown on backpack packing and tutorials on traveling in foreign countries. My daywear for travel started with my Girl Scout uniform. Once in Canada, we were in camps and regular clothing was the norm. But traveling … it was always the uniform to announce who we were.

The provinces of Manitoba and Ontario were our first stops. While we were in Manitoba, the person who was to cart us around was Miss Hoskin, who became a highlight in my life. I remember her as a craggy older woman with hairs on her chin and a cigarette hanging from her lips, aways lighting one after another. She was also high ranking in the Canadian Girl Guides, as they call Girl Scouts in Canada. When she would appear at different locations for inspections, everyone would be "quivering in her boots." We heard that often. But as we spent hours traveling with her in her car, we developed quite a camaraderie. We teased Miss Hoskin a lot, which nobody else would dare to do. At the end of our time with her, we were in tears, even Miss Hoskin.

One place she took us was to the northernmost city in Manitoba called Flin Flon, which is situated along the Manitoba-Saskatchewan border. It's named after the fictional adventurer/explorer hero in a book written in 1905. Flin Flon is a small city built on rock with all the sidewalks made of wooden paths. Being there was my first and only experience in seeing the Northern Lights— eerie and fascinating, going in and out, waving back and forth like some kind of computer light show. What was in front of me was a kaleidoscope of amazing colors: blues, greens, pinks, purples, and white. I loved it.

We were taken to a camp for older, experienced Guides down near the Minnesota border on one of the beautiful lakes. While there, they arranged a "Wide Game." This was a series of competing events to measure the abilities of Guides' knowledge of camping in the wilderness. We were to participate and they were anxious to show us that their skills were superior to ours.

Well, to their surprise, the outcome was that Bonnie, Patty Jo and I scored the top three of all the participants and I scored the highest. At one station, the instructions were to build a fire and boil water as quickly as possible. Nearby was a pile of wood, a barrel of water, and a bucket to put water in to boil. The only instructions were to boil water as quickly as possible. Where the others filled their buckets, I put barely an inch of water in the bucket, placing it on the fire I had built. Voila. In less than a minute, my water boiled. Task completed.

During our time in Canada, we stayed with a different family almost every night. We had delightful experiences with all of these Canadians and learned an enormous amount about their families, their beliefs, their customs, and their lives. The only downside was that every night, the family for that night cooked their absolute best meal and insisted that we try everything. We were quickly gaining weight!

When we had time to ourselves, we became as close as sisters, sharing our own lives with each other. We read the letters from our boyfriends to each other and gave each other advice on how to answer those letters! We laughed a lot. It was a wonderful time.

Lynn's letters to me were filled with amorous declarations, such as: "Don't ever forget how much I love you. I continually dream about having you as my wife, of us in a home and a family of our own." I thought a lot about him and realized that he was a very smart person, as well as entertaining, interesting, and fun to be with. I decided to give him more encouragement when I got back. Bonnie and Patty Jo approved.

Back to School

When we got back to school, Lynn and I were so happy to see each other. We started spending a lot of time together, but I still wasn't making any commitments.

He had joined a non-Greek fraternity called The Vikings. As a sophomore, I was a monitor at a Libby Dorm, a freshman women's dorm. Studying together became the norm in the living space of the dorm. Back in our own spaces, we spent a lot of phone time later in the evening. Lynn's objective was to convince me to become his steady girlfriend.

One evening we went out to have a drink at the "Sink." He had a beer and I had my usual 7-Up. He was talking about something and then out of the blue he said, "I would drop dead if you ever agreed to be my girlfriend." And I replied, "Where do you want to be buried?"

> **If that house could talk, we would have been the genesis of a sitcom.**

He continued to talk about something else and I interrupted him with "Wait a minute! YOU said, 'I would drop dead if you ever agreed to be my girlfriend' and I responded saying, 'Where do you want to be buried?'" He looked blankly at me for a bit and then finally got it. He was in ecstasy! So, I got pinned with his Viking pin while his fraternity serenaded me. Everything about that evening was wonderful.

Where I lived in a dorm, Lynn lived in a house with two of his close friends, Chuck Angevine and Bill Daney.

If that house could talk, we would have been the genesis of a sitcom. What fun and adventures we had along with Chuck and Bill's girlfriends. Both of his buddies were brilliant and eventually graduated Suma Cum Laude. Chuck went on to become an Ambassador and Bill became a physician. One time, he told us how four people had to share a cadaver. He didn't like it that he had to watch someone else cut into a hand instead of learning it for himself. Right then and there, I made up my mind that when I go, I want my body donated to the University of Colorado Medical Center to support the education of medical students.

Lynn and I decided to get married between my junior and senior year in my hometown of Rapid City. Our honeymoon would be bicycling across Europe during the summer.

We had so much fun making all of our plans. When we told my parents, my father was furious. "I have spent all this money for you to get a college education, and now you're going to get married and have kids and not finish college!" It took a

He wrote the most romantic love letters!

long time to convince him that I was going to finish college. And Lynn still had several years to finish his PhD. And I promised him that if I didn't finish college, I would pay him back every cent he had spent on my four years of schooling. Finally, he calmed down.

I spent the summer between my sophomore and junior year staying in Rapid City working in Dad's office. He designed and built homes for first time home buyers. I didn't enjoy the work much but Lynn and I were going to need the money I was earning. Most of the time, I did little but answer the phone; gave sales talks for homes that were tiny with no garages or basements; showed homes to customers; and kept the books. I did nothing that I needed a college degree for.

Lynn came to visit a couple of times and in between, he wrote the most romantic love letters! These years that Lynn mastered the art of romancing became the first in a series of incidents that helped me overcome my feelings of being inferior. He would constantly tell me how beautiful I was and how smart. Well, I knew I was smart, but I had a hard time believing I was beautiful. I had a mirror, after all! All I could ever see in that mirror was a Plain Jane with freckles. I have beautiful auburn hair. Bit by bit, I started feeling better about myself.

During spring break, we drove back to Lynn's hometown so I could meet his parents, and they me. Amos Dewitt Wilson and Delia Von Haldy Wilson lived on farmland just west of Clinton, Michigan. They were strict Quakers who didn't believe in smoking, drinking, card playing, dancing or shows. I was wondering how they would fit in with my family. But as it turned out, everything at the wedding went fine with them.

Well, Lynn was nothing like his parents! Their religion was forced on him so hard that he rebelled. And even though they didn't approve of his lifestyle, he remained their favorite son. It came about this way: After they had been married for a few years and no children had come along, they joined with several other families from the church to help out a family who had twelve children and no way to take care of them. So, the church families stepped into help and adopted them. Lynn's parents adopted two–Arnold and Annabelle. All of the children had names that started with "A"!

Sometime later, Delia told how she was sitting at her piano one day and an angel came and spoke to her and told her she would have a son. She was filled with tremendous joy. Soon, she became pregnant with Lynn and then later, Paul. Of the four children, Lynn remained their favorite.

Suddenly, June was here and we were preparing for a wedding!

4
Wedding and Honeymoon

We were thrilled with Dad's surprise wedding gift.

Surrounded by friends and family, it was a happy time at the Methodist Church in Rapid City, South Dakota. Lynn and I married on June 16, 1957.

The wedding was beautiful. Mom created my dress for me that was beautiful. And then the excitement really started.

We were thrilled with Dad's surprise wedding gift a few days before our big day—a '54 Chevy.

Ready for the wedding

We hid it in a neighbor's garage and in our excitement, we told Lynn's closest friends about it. They were excited, too … and in a frenzy to find where it was.

Finally, Dad spilled the beans … telling them where the car was.

> **With a roll of wide white tape, he closed the wound.**

Lynn's brother Paul snuck into the room where Lynn's things were and took the car keys out of Lynn's pants set out for our get-away that first night to the Black Hills. Paul along with Lynn's closest friends who were all in the wedding party set about decorating it.

Lynn grabbed the keys of one of the guys to bargain with to get ours back. What followed could have been in a Charlie Chaplin movie. Lynn and Paul got in a scrap over the keys, wrestling with headlocks. Suddenly, Paul's head butted Lynn's chin, splitting it to the bone. His beautiful rented white jacket now spouted crimson blood down the front.

Dad came to the rescue. With a roll of wide white tape, he closed the wound, and redirected Lynn and the boys back to the house. The guys were quite remorseful, especially brother Paul.

The Honeymoon

Our honeymoon destination was Europe: a six-week bicycling adventure that we had started planning the moment we decided to marry. It began on the Johan Von Oldenbarnevelt, a student ship where we sailed from New York to Southampton, England. Being a student ship at that time, it meant no cohabitation. Lynn's roommates knew we were newlyweds and made ample time so that we could be alone. That first week was a bit of a challenge for us. But heck, it was cheap. We were young. And Europe awaited us.

We spent the first day in *S'Hampton*, as the locals called it, finding the bicycles we had bought on arrival, getting them fixed up with a different gear shift, and what we needed for our grand trek. It took us quite a while to figure out how to pack all our stuff on the bicycles. What we quickly realized was that we had *too much stuff*. Our tent poles and stakes were the first to go.

Our early exploration in preplanning told us that hostels would be a fabulous way to connect with other young people from many different countries. The first was the Winchester Youth Hostel. It introduced us to bunk beds, sleeping in them using our sleeping bags on top of the thin mattress; and meals served on a long table. We tried to stay in hostels all along the way. The only drawback was that we couldn't sleep together when we stayed there!

Sometimes, at the end of our day, none were in range, so we had to pay for a hotel. You may be thinking, *Carol Ann, why would you want to stay in a hostel. You are just married?* Well, we were students still. Money was minimal. Those hostels usually charged 25 to 50 cents per night to sleep there and about 50 cents for breakfast and dinner. You may be thinking, *that's not much.* It was for us. We both watched every nickel we spent.

In London, we discovered that Lawrence Olivier, Vivian Leigh and Anthony Quayles were starring in a play. We knew nothing about it, but it was Olivier, Leigh, and Quayles. It had to be amazing. We treated ourselves and saw "Titus Andronicus" by Shakespeare. We even had a box all to ourselves. It was terrific! And it was the bloodiest thing we had ever seen! Everyone in the cast was killed except one. We felt a little out of place because everyone else was really dressed up, but we didn't care.

France was our next stop via the Night Ferry that was our transport, bringing us to Ostend. Once landed, we bicycled in northern France, slowly getting to Paris. Once there, we boarded the bike-friendly Metro, with our sights set for Notre Dame. Finding a hostel, we left out bikes and set out for the cathedral.

For a girl who was immersed in Montana and the Dakotas growing up, walking into Notre Dame was overwhelming: the beauty, the space, the windows, the architecture … everything. I had never seen anything like it. We were especially impressed with the rose windows.

From the cathedral, we walked downtown to the Arc de Triomphe. It was like a magnet for us. Sitting on a little hill, it can be easily seen from all around. We went to the top and got a beautiful view of Paris and marveled at the twelve streets that were the spokes in a circle around the Arc. From here, we walked to the Palais de Chaillot and the Eiffel Tower. Again, the architecture and structure pulled us in … so beautiful! From the top of the Eiffel Tower, you have an expansive view of lawns, parks, and the heart of Paris below.

Germany would be our next destination. After five days in France, we were off to Hamburg on a bright and early morning. Before we got there, we cycled to Darmstadt where the saga of the flat tire continued. It was flat tire number three. This time it was Lynn's tire. There we found a hostel filled with American kids who were on tours.

> It was an eye-opener for us.

As we listened to their stories, we both felt pretty good that we chose to do it "our way." Where they ordered a typical American fare of steaks and salads, we immersed ourselves in all things local. They revealed that their tours cost them a total of $850, and that didn't include the cost of their boat fare.

It was an eye-opener for us. The Americans were often loud and pushy. Quickly, we saw how the Americans make such bad impressions on Europeans. The Americans insisted on being served before others could get breakfast. We even heard their tour guides telling others that they couldn't sit down at tables until all their American clients were seated. Sometimes, Lynn and I were ashamed to admit we, too, were Americans.

Glad to leave them behind, our wheels headed to Hamburg and specifically the Dreckmanns, a family Lynn knew well. He was excited; he had wonderful connections here. When he was in high school, he was an exchange student to Germany. Most of his senior year was spent living with the Dreckmanns. They were like his second family. Wealthy, they own many acres of land in the country that is now surrounded by Hamburg. The family bred horses, and the grounds had many horses, and a huge riding arena where lessons were given. Besides their large mansion, they owned apartment buildings, factories, and a pub at the entrance of their property.

Mrs. Dreckmann welcomed us with open arms into her home. We were given a suite of rooms and made ourselves at home. A delicious raspberry drink was brought to us while we read our mail. Before we knew it, we heard a gong—the call to supper. The meal was delicious, ending with cream of wheat, a common dessert.

One morning, Mrs. Dreckmann showed us her beautiful dishes and silver. She said that at one time, she had 55 people staying there. She has several sets of china and silver, enough settings for 24 to 40 people. After the meals here, everyone joins hands and says *Mahlzeit*, a German salutation meaning blessed mealtime. Also, everyone shakes hands good morning, hello, goodbye and good night. Goodness! At meals, they must have their hands above the table at all times. That comes from an old tradition that will show that you are not hiding any weapons.

We were at the Dreckmanns for two wonderful weeks in August 1957. During that time, we were taken to many places, too many to mention. And we enjoyed being entertained by the whole family, which consisted of six children: Peter, Elizabeth, Hans Holger, Karston, Adelheid, and Angelica. We both felt sad to leave; something we had put off.

> I had to fix my flat, again.

But before we could leave, I had to fix my flat, again. Then we loadied up and started out. We were thankful for the food Mrs. Dreckmann sent with us. At the end of the day, we found ourselves setting up camp by flashlight. Thoroughly exhausted after a long ride, we fell into our sleeping bags. A day's ride could range anywhere from ten miles when lots of hills were involved to eighty miles when it was flat. The next morning, it was difficult to vacant our sleeping bags. And this time, it was Lynn's turn to fix a flat tire before we could be off to the next hostel.

Holland was a new destination and it wasn't at all like we expected. There were many hills and pine forests and the biggest surprise was the superhighways exclusively for bicycles! Encountering strong winds, we finally stopped in a forest for some protection. While I set up camp, Lynn went into Ede for food supplies: bread, cheese, wurst, and apple juice.

Snuggled in our sleeping bags, we were abruptly wakened by the sounds of army maneuvers! Our campsite was smack in the middle of an Army practice ground and tanks were headed our way! We broke camp in a hurry and pedaled as fast as we could.

Once again, my tire wasn't behaving. Across Europe, it had gone flat more times that I have fingers. After supper, Lynn patched two more holes in my tire—12 by now. With our six weeks coming to end, we decided not to spend our last dollars on new tires. The bikes would not be going back with us. And I for one was glad to leave them behind. The last thing I bought was for my dad. A pair of wooden shoes went home with us.

It was time to head home and return to school to fulfill my promise to my father. I would complete my degree. We knew every penny we had spent abroad and the cost to get there and back. It came to a grand total of $500 for the two of us for six weeks in Europe! Not bad.

5
School and Babies

Before my 21st birthday, I had accomplished
four major events in my life.

What an adventure Lynn and I had, loving every minute of it. And we loved each other. We were actually drunk with love.

Immediately, we were back at school. It was my senior year and Lynn was starting his PhD program in chemistry. His research work was pretty exciting, what with explosions taking place in the lab. We were excited for what lay ahead for the two of us and our first year together. It was 1957.

Then, the unexpected happened. Lynn was excited. I wasn't so sure. We figured it happened just before we left Europe. Oh no! I was pregnant. It wasn't supposed to happen this soon. What if my dad was right? Well, he didn't know his daughter and wouldn't be right because I would finish my senior year and graduate in June.

I've always been a list maker. If there was a time to get out the paper and pen, this was it. We lived in a very small studio apartment. We had a couch that pulled out into a bed, an efficiency kitchen, and a tiny bathroom. *The place was meant for just one person, certainly not three! At the top of my list was posted "married housing."* Within a few months, we had a two-bedroom unit for $45 a month, and thankfully, it included all our utilities. With Lynn's salary of $60 a month, we became minimalists with our needs.

As my pregnancy advanced, I knew what was going on in my body … but few did. Being tall, just our closest friends and family knew I was pregnant. Visually, even my neighbors and students were clueless. When I disappeared one afternoon and people asked where I was, Lynn responded, "She's in the hospital having a baby." They were astounded not knowing any birth was imminent.

> When my name was called, we all shouted out.

Cheryl Lynn Wilson arrived weighing only 4 pounds, 9 ounces on May 18, 1958. She was so tiny! At birth, she didn't breathe right away and needed help. She had to stay in the hospital for two additional weeks and got out just in time for my graduation ceremony!

The ceremony was held outdoors in beautiful Colorado weather in early June. The official "walk" was quite a distance for me, just having given birth a few weeks earlier. I had thought Lynn could hold baby Cheryl in stadium seats, but we scratched that idea. Instead, I became an observer, sitting with my family. When my name was called, we all shouted out.

Cheryl was misdiagnosed initially. Later, she was diagnosed as having spastic hemiplegia, which means that the muscles on her right side were tighter than the ones on her left. When she was two, she got braces on her legs that really helped her even though she teetered like a drunk when she walked! We constantly had to do exercises to stretch and strengthen her muscles. Oh, how she hated that and it made me feel like a bad mother because of the crying and screaming as I worked on retraining her muscles! It was a constant battle between the two of us as I would stretch her muscles.

In the meantime, another unexpected surprise came our way. Scott Eric Wilson debuted on November 18, 1959. This time, others did note that I was pregnant.

Now, I had two babies in diapers, which meant lots of wash days. I would pull the wringer washer out of its niche and fill it with water from the hose attached to the faucet. Add soap. Wash for ten minutes. Then put them through the wringer. I was fortunate to have the newer wringer that worked electronically instead of having to crank it by hand. Next was emptying the washer and filling it again with clean water. Put clothes in and agitate for ten minutes. Wring them out again. Empty washer. Take clothes outside to hang them from the clothesline with clothespins. A brief breeze in Boulder would dry them in less than a half hour. Then take clothes down, fold, and I was set until the next wash day.

With my growing family and Lynn in school plus working part-time, I decided I needed to bring in some income. Like many women in the workforce at that time … selling Tupperware was common. I could sell and sell I did, making enough to make the payments on a used car for us.

It was a confidence builder for me. Another boost came with my Tupperware experience. Each week, prizes were dangled to all the dealers as added incentives. The goal was to present at enough parties sponsored by a hostess that would bring in lots of sales. Then, prizes would come our way.

Typically, prizes weren't much to write home about. But one week, out came a walnut teacart. Oh, I coveted that teacart in the worst way! It had a removable serving tray that lifted up out of the top. I was determined to win it; and win it, I did! There was some kind of jolt that came with winning it. I realized that I had the ability to accomplish whatever I wanted. What a realization! That was the second event that helped build back confidence in myself.

When Lynn took his prelim exams, only three people passed out of the twenty-one who took them. Lynn was one of the three. We felt great about that. Then came comps and then orals and then he had to write his thesis. This all took a few years, graduating with a PhD in fluorine chemistry in 1961.

This was also the year that Mom and Dad applied to host a foreign student. My sister, Mary Margaret, would be a senior in high school that year. Their student was Joan Schwencke from Holland and what a delight she was! She fit right in at high school. Everyone loved her. The girls became like sisters and a lifelong relationship was formed. Her parents came over here, my parents went over there, Joan and her husband came over here, she came over here multiple times, and I visited her every time I went to Europe.

When I said we became like a family to the Schwenckes, I wasn't kidding. Joan and I figured we have gone back and forth quite a few times. Finally, we created a log to see what our travels had been over the years.

My sister Mary Margaret with exchange student Joan Schwencke

1960-61	Joan was an exchange student with my family in South Dakota.
1962	My sister, Mary Margaret, visits Joan in Holland for two months.
1964	Joan's parents visit my family in South Dakota for six weeks.
1967	My parents visit Joan's family in Holland for three weeks.
1968	Joan and husband Hans visit my family in South Dakota for three weeks.
1971	Joan visits my family in South Dakota for three weeks.
1973	Mary Margaret visits Joan in Holland for three weeks.
1974	Cheryl and I visit with Joan in Holland for one week.
1975	Scott and I visit with Joan in Holland for one week.
1978	Marie and I visit with Joan in Holland for one week.
2000	Bill and I visit with Joan in Holland for four days.
2001	Joan visits Bill and I in Longmont, Colorado, for a week.
2012	Carol Ann and Sonny visit Joan in Holland for four days.

Before my 21st birthday, I had accomplished four major events in my life: got married, bicycled across Europe, had a baby, and graduated from college.

6
New Beginning and New Trials

At my six-month checkup, it was not good news.

After interviewing with several companies, Lynn was hired by 3M in St. Paul, Minnesota, with a starting salary of $6,500. Remember, this was six decades ago! Back then, in 1961, we felt we were rich! Now instead of waiting for the next bit of money showing up, I could pay bills when they came in. In 2022, fluorine chemists with a PhD would be looking at a minimum of $150,000 a year.

We located to White Bear Lake, Minnesota, and built a house for around $20,000. We moved into our new house in 1962 adding new furniture and decorating. Cheryl had her first corrective surgery on her leg that put her into a cast when she was four. We were trying to straighten those muscles. Then, surprise … another baby!

I was pregnant with Marie and was trying to explain this to Cheryl, age 6.

Mom: The baby is in my tummy.

Cheryl: In there?

M: Yes, it's growing and getting bigger and then I'll go to the hospital and Dr. G. will take it out.

C: Out of your mouth?

M: No, he'll take it out someplace else.

C: Will he broke you and then sew you up with needle and thread?

M: Maybe.

C: No, he won't broke you. You're too tight. Is the baby crying in there?

M: No, the baby's just sleeping.

C: (Derisively) The baby isn't in your tummy!

M: It isn't? Where is it?

C: It's at the hospital. You go to the hospital to pick it up.

M: Okay.

C: Is the baby really in there?

M: Yes, we let the baby grow in here until big enough to take out and put in a crib.

C: Do you look like a crib?

M: (laughs)

C: The baby isn't in there!

M: It isn't?

C: NO

Marie Michelle Wilson was born on February 15, 1963. We were on top of the world.

The summer after she was born, I wasn't feeling well at all. No wonder, I was actually diagnosed with ulcerative colitis. That fall, I went into the hospital for a checkup and discovered that a malignant tumor was in my colon. Surgery was immediately scheduled. This was scary. I had three kids under the age of five. Thankfully, all my neighbors had kids and pitched in to help me during recovery. Of course, my mother was there as well. It was who she was. At my six-month checkup, it was not good news. More cancer was identified, so more surgery to remove more of the colon.

As time went on, I was back to my busy schedule. And because I had been an exchange Scout in the past, I was in charge of the selection committee who would choose the girls who would participate in the trips the following summer. This included a luncheon for 24 committee members to choose a nominee for an exchange Girl Scout. We had dinners that would include the girls who had applied plus members of the committee. We were looking at the cream of the crop and it was a humbling experience. What difficult decisions we had to make! They were all exceptional young people. It made for crowded dinners at my house but it was a wonderful experience.

Of course, my participating in art fairs, going to the theater, starting a ceramics class, knitting three sweaters in time for Christmas, teaching a Sunday school class, and hosting a Halloween party were all part of my life.

> **It was a riot and a huge success.**

I've always loved to have others over and cooking. One night, we hosted a "Yankee Trader Dinner" with thirteen of our friends. Food was prepared in advance and placed in boxes—entrees, salads, and desserts. Each person had to choose three boxes, not knowing what was in any of them. They might end up with two desserts and a salad and no entree. Next was the trade with Monopoly money! They could trade around using play money to get what they wanted to eat.

One guest asked, "Would you pass the olives?"

Another would respond, even with items that were openly available on the table like the olives, "Are they worth a dollar to you?"

If person said yes, an exchange would be made. There were olives for money … rolls for money … pasta salad for money … fried chicken for money.

One friend bought the basket of rolls from me for $100 and then went around saying, "Who wants a roll? Only $20 each!"

Her husband said, "I just don't understand my wife. She's not like this at home!" But she was a shrewd trader at this party.

And at the conclusion, play money was used to bid on prizes.

It was a riot and a huge success. Someone said, "How can we have the Wilsons over for dinner after this?"

And oh yes, we applied for and were accepted to host a Macalester foreign student. His name was Wolfgang Kuhne from Germany. We had such fun with him. He really enjoyed our kids and he was glad that Lynn and I turned out to be a young couple. He said that most of the people who asked for a foreign student were much older as they wanted someone the same age as their college son or daughter. Wolfgang was interested in the same things we were: classical music, jazz, theater, skiing, camping, fishing and more. We spent a lot of our time together laughing and comparing the linguistics of our languages.

We asked Wolfgang to come out Friday for supper so he could see us decorated for Christmas before he left to go East for vacation. I asked him if we should have our tree all up before he got here and he asked, "Don't Americans usually trim the tree as a family?" I said yes and he replied, "Well, we better trim it as a family then!" Lynn and I cut the tree in readiness of his arrival. He helped us trim it and then stayed overnight.

The early sixties were good for all of us. Lynn loved his work with 3M. With three kids, my hands were full and my energy was ebbing. In 1966, the doctors said I had not healed up the way I should have since my surgery two years earlier with their declaration that my insides were still raw and inflamed. The possibility of leading to more cancer was a concern. Then, after many trials and errors of radical changes to diet, new meds, and rest (ha … with three kids!) to bring me back to health … it didn't. The result was more surgery, resulting in an ileostomy.

This was quite a shock and took me quite a while to get used to handling it. For Lynn, he just took it in stride. I was 29 years old at this time. I was young for such a procedure. I had many concerns:

What about my clothes?

Would I have to get new ones that were different?

What would people think when they learned I had one?

Would people be able to see it? Would it look like I had a bottle under my clothes?

What about my sex life?

I found out later that these fears seemed to be what all women ostomates had. Men were different. They worried first of all about sex and second about the clothes factor!

> **Lynn could hardly get it off of me to go to bed!**

It turned out that after I healed from the surgery and was able to get back to a somewhat normal life, clothes were not the issue. Over fifty years have passed since that surgery. As I look back, I'm grateful that I had the doctor that I had. As a specialist in a field that was radically changing with new methods of treatment, care, and appliances, he was in the right place at the time I needed his skills.

Fortunately, I had a visitor from the local ostomy association who had had the same surgery. She helped me with all my questions and she looked so normal! She showed me that life could go on as usual. Later, I learned that in the US alone, over 200,000 people per year had ostomy surgery. This included colostomy, ileostomy, and urostomy. It became the surgery that "nobody talks about." It's not unusual for people to become reclusive, limit their socializing, and feel that their life has ended.

It was summertime and the outdoors called to us. We had plans to go on an outing at the beach with friends so I went shopping for a bathing suit, finding one I loved. As I headed to the dressing room I thought, *I'll just try it on. No one has to know. I'm sure I won't be able to buy this one. I'll need one with a little skirt.* Looking in the mirror, I was elated. I called the clerk into the dressing room and asked excitedly, "Can you see anything?"

"What?" was her response.

"Can you *see* anything?" She had no idea about what I was talking. Well, I bought it, went home, put it back on, and danced around the house with joy! Lynn could hardly get it off of me to go to bed!

The Political Scene

We became interested in politics and hosted several lunches, coffees and evening events for candidates running for office. One time, we hosted a pig roast for Clark MacGregor, our local candidate for Congress. We put up tent awnings in the yard and strung banners and added flaming tiki torches set around the yard and Christmas tree lights in the trees. Our backyard was quite a scene, roasting the pig as it turned on a spit. The aromas were fantastic and the taste of the succulent outcome was the talk of the town. With over 125 attending, it got a lot of attention. We really knew how to throw a party! And I sure learned a lot about what went on "behind the scenes."

A few years later we were again campaigning for a candidate who was running for state office, Steve Maxwell. This time it was a beer and pretzel party at our home. He dropped by to talk to us for about an hour and then left to go to the next event. The way these guys campaigned was really something. He got up at 5 a.m., was at the factory gate by 6 a.m. to shake hands with the workers changing shifts, attended coffee parties, luncheons, business meetings, shopping centers, and attended six more coffee parties in the evening! Later we had a second party for Steve. I guess we were the only ones to ever serve beer instead of coffee and we became quite well-known for that fact. People would say, "Oh yes, you're the ones who had the beer and pretzel party." One person made a comment ... I heard that this is the "beer brawl" that Steve was at all night!

Lynn and I became quite involved with the Young Republican League. In fact, Lynn was elected chairman of the group and I became membership chair. For a few years, this was a big part of our lives. There were district conventions, county conventions, campaigning, and learning about the new bills. We hosted many meetings and parties at our home. One big event for us was attending the Governor's Ball: long dresses, black tuxes, finest jewelry—it was quite a spectacle that unfolded.

Since that time, I changed my party affiliation to Independent and have voted for both Democrats and Republicans, depending on the situation and the candidate.

The Art Scene

A couple of our neighbors were artists and I started "dabbling" in art and some crafts. It was such fun. Mary and I started attending art shows in the area with our "art projects." She was a bona fide artist while I was consumed with making crafts and calling them art. We exhibited at the local art fairs. First, there were the "String Things," different colored threads sewn onto construction paper to make geometric patterns; then the Polish Wycinanki or Polish papercuts; then pottery and paintings. Lynn even painted a few canvases to take along. We always ended up selling a few things but not enough to cover our costs. Yet we loved doing it and I was caught up in the excitement and flair of it. Each summer we would attend five or six art fairs with our works. This carried on until my full-time profession of developing a pottery studio and a line of pottery that was sold nationally. Read more on that later.

This 'n That

One day, a couple knocked on our door inquiring about the lot across the street. They were interested in building on it and wanted to ask about the neighborhood. We found out they had been in Boulder the same time we had and he and Lynn had taught chemistry in the chem department at the same time. He had just come to work for 3M and was working in the same building as Lynn! Talk about coincidences! They were Ken and Marge King who had five children. Marge became my closest friend.

Looking back at our life in White Bear Lake, I am amazed at how busy we were. Constantly throwing parties, going to other parties, getting involved with organizations like the political party and the Beaux Arts Center, Girl Scouts, skiing expeditions, and taking classes. Oh yes, we had also hosted a foreign student.

> It felt as though we were in heaven.

We vacationed many times together. Along with skiing, we had several experiences camping at Madeline Island, located off the north shore of Wisconsin in Lake Superior. We would take the ferry across to the island, carry our tent and supplies way down the shore so we would be past all the other campers. Then, we would set up our double tent and proceed to relax. Lynn was the best sandcastle builder, while the kids collected rocks and waded in the lake. I excelled at campfire cooking. It felt as though we were in heaven. We also had a marvelous trip to San Francisco, another to Disneyland with the kids, and another to Montana for fun.

Lynn and I experienced the elegance of the "rich and famous" when we attended the Beaux Arts Ball in Minnetonka. I had joined the art association earlier and this was their annual costume ball. We went as two pirates and if I do say so myself, we were darling! Lynn wore a white shirt open to the waste with the collar tucked under and a red sash with his

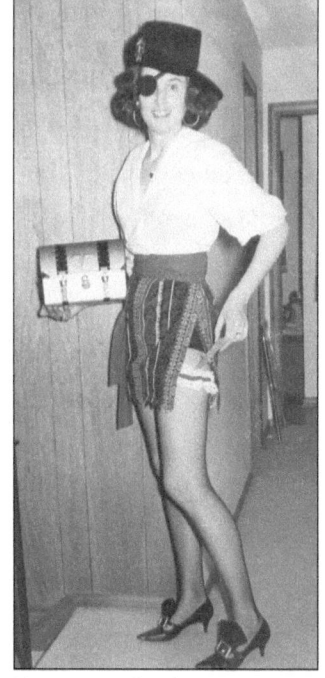
My costume for the Beaux Arts Ball.

black pants. He had a bright scarf tied around his head, long painted on sideburns, an eye patch and one big gold hoop earring.

I got a pair of black net stockings and wore black heels with big gold buckles attached. My ragged miniskirt was slit up to the waist on one side with a garter that had a stiletto tucked into it. I had on a white blouse with puffy sleeves and a big black hat with one side pinned up with a large brooch. Then I bought a lunch bucket, sprayed it gold, added black tape with painted gold rivets and a black lock. That was my treasure chest which served as my purse for the evening.

There were about 200 people at the ball but only about half of them wore costumes. The rest were in tuxedos and long gowns. After a fabulous dinner, there was dancing. We met so many interesting and wonderful people.

Before the Ball, Janet Riggs had a cocktail party at her home, so we were able to meet others who were going to the Ball. She lived in an old Victorian mansion and when we drove up to it, I saw no other cars and I thought, "Oh no, don't tell me we are the first ones here!" Well, we pulled up by the door and all of a sudden there was a man standing there saying, "May I park your car?" Well, the next day I felt I had just been to Cinderella's Ball!

Have you ever heard a random comment that resonated with you forever? Well, at the Ball, one of the gentlemen came up to me and commented on my amazingly beautiful legs. I wasn't used to this kind of flattery and I was a little flustered and stammered out my thanks that went way overboard. He then said, "You know, my wife is very beautiful and often gets comments on her beauty. She just tosses off a 'thank you' as if it isn't a big deal. That's the way you handle it with grace." I knew that I had just heard some good advice.

With my years of travel—sometimes solo for business, sometimes with a friend, sometimes with family members—my memories are often woven with the words of Jan Struthers in her classic, *Mrs. Miniver*.

> …for when you first come home from a strange place you are always something of a ghost. They were sorry when you went away, and they welcome you back with affection; but in the meanwhile, they have adjusted their lives a little to your absence. For the first meal or two, there is not quite enough room for your chair. They ask, "Where did you go? What was it like?" but for the life of you, you cannot tell them. You can say, "It was like a large, neat Scotland;" or "They trim all their buildings with wooden lace;" or "There was a nice little German boy staying at the pension;" or "I made friends with a charming farmer at the village fete." But however eagerly they listen, they do not really take in what you are saying. For you cannot make them understand the essential point, which is that when you went away you took the centre of the universe with you, so that the whole thing went on revolving, just as usual, round your own head. How could they, indeed, be expected to believe this, when they know quite well that all the time the centre of everything stayed at home with them? It is a day or two, as a rule, before your universe and theirs (like the two images in a photographic range finder) merge and become concentric: and when that happens, you know you are really home.

Kid Talk

Television personality Art Linkletter made a living saying, "Kids say the darndest things." My kids were no different. One morning, I had just about had it with their bickering and carrying on. Yelling at them hadn't helped. Finally, I said, "What do you think God thinks when He hears you talking to each other that way?"

Cheryl at 8½, Scott at 7 and Marie at 4 had quite a discussion. It became my Art Linkletter moment.

Marie: God can't hear us because he's up in heaven.

Scott: Is heaven beyond space?

Marie: When I was at Ryan's house, he told me that the Devil lives under the ground.

Scott: There isn't any room for the Devil under the ground because the earth is made up of rock.

Cheryl: The whole earth is not made up of rock.

Scott: It is too because my teacher told me so.

Cheryl: Well, we're studying the earth and I know it isn't.

Scott: Well, you don't know what I know because *you're not me!*

Do any of you do family letters? My mom and dad each came from large families and from the time I was small, I knew that they each did family letters. Each person would put their letter in and send the packet of letters on to the next in line. When it came back, they would take their letter out and enclose a new one. So, when my sister, brother and I were all married, we decided it was time for us to have our own family letter with our parents. Over the years, I saved all my letters. Therefore, I don't have to depend on my memory for everything!

In July 1967, through a program called Operation Goodwill, we had two underprivileged girls with us for two weeks. From broken homes with drinking problems, they were both extroverts and the house was wild during their stay with us! Cheryl's room became their sleeping spot, each on an air mattress.

With a total of five kids under one roof, I tried to find enough things to do to keep them busy. We went swimming, went to a play, played on the balcony, made things from alphabet jewelry, went on an alphabet hike, a coin hike, went for treats, and went to the library. Dishonesty surfaced a few times, something Cheryl just couldn't understand and was quite puzzled by the whole thing. It's bad enough for something to be missing in the first place, but then if everyone denies taking it, it must have just disappeared because as Cheryl knows, you just don't lie about things.

We were glad when the time was over and the girls left us. But looking back at the experience, I'm glad we did it and would do it again because we all learned a lot. And I hoped the two girls did as well.

> I called it Carol Ann's Goop.

One of Lynn's colleagues was from Italy. Only in the States for a year, he had a problem sometimes with our language. He asked Lynn what it meant when someone would say, "Jeet jet?" and the other would answer, "No jew?" Lynn laughed and explained that the first comment was "Did you eat yet?" and the answer was "No, did you?" And then there was "Scome." Lynn explained they were saying "Let's go home."

Have you ever had one of those days? One night I was going to fix hamburgers in a special, delicious way that Lynn liked so well. I knew I didn't have buns, but I figured Lynn could run and get them when he came home. Then I found out that I also didn't have any Lipton's onion soup. But I found a package of sloppy joe mix, so I decided that we would have that instead. I started browning the meat and added the sloppy joe powder. Then I went to get the tomato sauce and discovered I didn't have any so I added canned tomatoes. Then I thought it looked more like chili than sloppy joes so I decided to add some kidney beans. Well, I didn't have any so I added pork 'n beans. It certainly was different and definitely not the special hamburger that Lynn had expected. I called it Carol Ann's Goop.

7
The Big Move

Lynn was quite the expert of spit pig roasting.

As much as we liked our time in White Bear Lake, Lynn and I were constantly wishing we could return to Boulder, Colorado. The Minnesota winters were brutal and the snow never melted until late spring. The summers were hot and humid and filled with mosquitoes. Then Lynn heard that IBM was building a large facility in Boulder. He kept his eye on the progress and when the time came in September 1968, he applied for a position there.

Then … excitement! IBM contacted Lynn and offered him a job to start the first part of November 1968. We were ecstatic; 3M was not. The company was terribly unhappy that Lynn would be leaving. As one of the few company experts in his field, it took two men to replace him.

Marge shared in my excitement, exclaiming that now they could snowbird with us. Her husband had attended the University of Colorado and would later attend reunions, staying with us. Of course, when I would need to be in Colorado before we moved, the kids would stay with her.

> It was time for the final tree ceremony.

Within a short time, I was in Boulder and found a house for us to rent on the corner of Martin Drive and Table Mesa Drive. It would be our temporary landing spot until we found acreage to eventually build on. Once there, we discovered Spanish Hills. Selecting an acre site, we started building our dream house. Eventually, we bought the adjacent acre that housed a barn along with a horse. What a wonderful place it was to live in. We all thrived. Every morning upon waking, we were greeted with the back range of the Continental Divide. We became close to our neighbors who had children the same ages as ours.

When building the house, we used the same German tradition we learned about on our honeymoon in Europe. When the highest rafters were put into place, a small fir tree was attached on top by one of the workers. It would collect all the good wishes and blessings from heaven. It would be taken down when the roof was added, to be kept for the final celebration upon completion of our new home.

When it was finished and had moved in, we had a big party. It was time for the final tree ceremony. We burned the little tree in our fireplace, surrounded with family, our new friends, and the workers who built our beautiful new home. That would assure that the good fortune would stay inside the house and keep out the evil spirits. Of course, everyone looked forward to the free beer!

We started meeting lots of people. We joined the New Neighbors Club. We met our Spanish Hills neighbors. We met Lynn's coworkers at IBM. And we started having company, lots of company! Our dear Minnesota friends didn't like the winters there either. And they knew our summertimes were glorious … and without mosquitoes. After all, what could be a better place to vacation than Boulder, Colorado, with free room and board? We loved seeing them again and again.

And within a year or two, I was involved with the Boulder Art Association. I was taking advanced pottery lessons that would lead to the formation of Carol Ann Pottery, Ltd., and I was the chair of the Ostomy Chapter in Denver.

In the spring of 1970, we had our Boundary Walking Party, also called Beating the Bounds, and Pig Roast. Boundary Walking is another old German tradition that would happen after someone bought a piece of land.

Wikipedia shares:

Beating the bounds is an ancient custom still observed in parts of England, Wales, and the New England region of the United States. In former times when maps were rare, it was usual to make a formal perambulation of the parish boundaries. Knowledge of the limits of each parish needed to be handed down so that such matters as liability to contribute to the repair of the church or the right to be buried within the churchyard were not disputed. The priest headed a crowd of boys who beat the parish boundary markers with green boughs, usually birch or willow. Sometimes the boys were whipped or violently bumped on the boundary stones to make them remember. The object of taking boys along is supposed to ensure that witnesses to the boundaries should survive as long as possible.

The ceremony had an important practical purpose. Checking the boundaries was a way of preventing encroachment by neighbors. Sometimes boundary markers would be moved or lines obscured, and a folk memory of the true extent of the parish was necessary to maintain integrity of borders by embedding knowledge in oral traditions.

The move was a huge success. That first year, the Boundary Walking Party included approximately 50 people. We gave each a trimmed branch to carry as he or she walked around our boundary. At each corner, one of my children would be stationed with trays of cheese and crackers or to refresh beers. It was such a hoot and everybody loved it. And I can't forget the pig roast. Yes, Lynn was quite the expert of spit pig roasting and everyone had more than a typical helping … with seconds requested. As people left, we were told over and over again that they looked forward to next year's celebration!

And they did with the pig roast hands down the star.

Lynn roasting the pig.

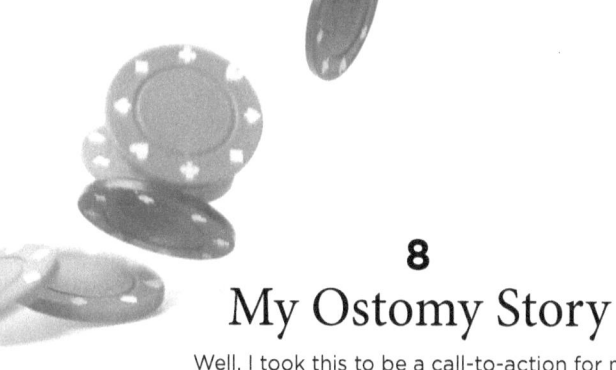

8
My Ostomy Story

Well, I took this to be a call-to-action for me!

The beginning of this story was in Chapter 5, *New Beginning and New Trials*, where I revealed my illness and the multiple surgeries I endured. With my schedule with kids and outside activities, having an ileostomy hadn't been on my calendar. Yet, it was. The good news … it didn't slow me down at all!

I had no idea how having this surgery was going to profoundly affect my life and the lives of millions going forward.

After we moved to Boulder, Colorado, I contacted the Colorado Ostomy Association located in Denver. The main purposes are to help rehabilitate other ostomates, to collect and exchange ideas and methods of rehabilitation, and to let doctors, nurses, and hospitals know this service is available.

At one of the first meetings I attended in the sixties, the speaker changed my life forever. Ira Karon was an elderly gentleman from Phoenix. My ears were buzzing as he told about countless cases where the doctors who performed the surgery didn't know how to tell their patients how to deal with it. The norm was to send the patient home with no instruction whatsoever. NONE! The patient would retire to bed and just stay there. Many never knew or learned about the variety of appliances to wear, ones that would allow them to live an active life. They would just keep mopping up the flow of shit that became the prominent feature of their "new" life.

Ira told us this was known as "the silent surgery." No one wanted to talk about it. That was so not me. As you know about my surgery, there is nothing an ostomate can't do if she, or he, has the proper appliance and knows how to take care of it. His words kept echoing to me. He said we—the ostomates— have a lot to do with educating the medical community. And that meant helping other patients, so they don't spend their lives around a bedpan.

In Phoenix, the ostomy group he belonged to had a visitation program so patients in the hospital had a visitor before ever going home. It makes all the difference in the world to know they are not alone and to hear about the normal life they can go back to.

Well, I took this to be a call-to-action for me! I became active with the club in Denver. Within a year, I was president and in the following year the membership had doubled. Monthly programs for members were fully attended. They wanted to hear and to share. It has been one of the most rewarding jobs I have ever done.

By now, some of you may be asking, "Just what is an ostomy?" So, I'll tell you.

> Ileostomy surgery is a life-saving procedure that allows bodily waste to pass through a surgically created stoma on the abdomen into a 'pouch' or 'ostomy bag' on the outside of the body. An ostomy may be necessary due to birth defects, cancer, inflammatory bowel disease, and many other medical conditions. My large intestine (the colon) was removed and the small intestine was brought through the abdominal wall to form a stoma. I wear a pouch which is emptied during the day.

A colostomy is created when a portion of the colon is removed and the remaining colon is brought to the abdominal wall. In this case, a bag is not needed and the ostomy is "irrigated" once a day.

A urinary ostomy is a general term for a surgical procedure which diverts urine away from a diseased or defective bladder. It results in a stoma and collection bag.

There are numerous well-known people with ostomies, including:

Marvin Bush, President George H. W. Bush's son

Dwight Eisenhower, General and President of the United States

William Powell, Actor

Rolf Benirschke, Place kicker for the San Diego Chargers who continued to play for seven years after he received his ileostomy

"Red" Skelton, Comedian and Actor

Fred Astaire, Actor and Dancer

Queen Elizabeth, the Queen Mother

I learned that in our five-state region, we were only the second club. It became my quest to start more clubs. I drove up to my hometown of Rapid City, South Dakota, where my parents still lived and started a club there. I discovered that one of my high school girlfriends also had an ileostomy, so our moms helped with promotion and organization of the new club. Next on my list included other sections of Colorado: Grand Junction, Greeley, Colorado Springs, and Pueblo.

And, of course, after starting each chapter, I would be one of the speakers and give a talk. I always told stories and everyone seemed to enjoy my presentations. This, and constantly speaking to nurses' groups on how to handle ostomy patients, was the background for my future speaking career.

I spoke at Grand Rounds at Saint Joseph Hospital in Denver, the 7 a.m. weekly meeting for doctors, and 87 attended.

With every presentation I delivered, I would reference appearance and always made it a point to wear slim clothes. The doctors thought the program was great with many supportive comments. Once I overheard a doctor say, "Where is it … in her heel?"

In 1970, our group hosted the Ostomy Regional Conference, and it was a tremendous success. Don Binder from the national board said he had never seen a better regional meeting. He took samples of our material and sent it out to all of the other groups in the US as an example of how to plan a regional meeting. My attendance at other regional meetings became routine and I attended the national convention each year. Soon, I was up for election to the national board.

> **Only her doctor knows for sure!**

In 1971, I began my first term on the board. At each convention, bids were taken from other cities for the next one. Rolling up my sleeves, I presented a bid for the 1974 National Convention to be held in Denver. And yes, we beat out the competition. Guess who was to be the chairman?!

In May 1972, I was invited to speak at a medical conference. My doctor, Dr. Waggoner, introduced me to the other attendees, saying, "Just wait till you hear this girl speak tomorrow. She is terrific!" That made me so worried about being *terrific* that I almost forgot my speech! But I wowed them and it was great fun.

Earlier, I had Lynn take a picture of me in my new slim bathing suit with the plunging neckline. Remember that Clairol commercial, "Does she or doesn't she? Only her hairdresser knows for sure!" I framed the picture of me and wrote across the bottom, "Does she or doesn't she? Only her doctor knows for sure!" I gave it to Dr. Waggoner and he loved it! He used it to show his patients and he shared it with other doctors.

At all of these meetings, I heard wonderful stories. Some of them brought tears to my eyes. Some were laugh-out-loud stories. And many were truly thought-provoking stories.

You know that children are the most adaptable people of all. They accept everything. They are curious at first, to be sure. But after they find out what it's all about, hah! So what?

One woman with an ileostomy had two little girls who figure that every mother has an ostomy, and when they grow up, they're going to have one, too!

The famous "Bathing Suit Picture."

Another little boy was hanging out the window talking to his friends. "I can't come out yet. My mom's not done irrigating yet. Is your mom finished with hers yet?"

One fellow with an ileostomy had a private pilot's license that he used in his business. During his surgery and recovery, he let his license lapse. After he became well again, he went back to reinstate his license which entailed taking a physical exam. The doctor had never seen an ostomate before. He wasn't sure exactly how to fill out the forms and how he could rate this gentleman for his license. So, he wrote to the district headquarters in Dallas and asked them how to handle the situation. Weeks went by and finally he got a letter back which said, "We have looked through all of our manuals and regulations and we can't find any place where it says that a pilot has to have a rectum."

One young mother had a body riddled with cancer. She proclaimed, "If I have a hole in my side so I can have a few months more to live, just who the hell should care if I have a hole in my side?!"

Several years ago, there was an article in the *Ann Landers* column that talked about ostomies. After it was published, our national office was flooded with over 1,400 letters. The following is the text from three such letters. And all these letters said the same thing: *Help!*

> *I'm from Chicago and I have an ostomy and I'm the only one in this area who has one and I'd like to talk to someone about it.*

> *I just found out that I have to have that kind of surgery, but I'd rather die first.*

> *My doctor operated on me and made a hole in my side and sent me home. It runs all the time and I spend all my time mopping it up and cleaning me up. Can you help me?*

I spoke to 500 doctors in Estes Park, Colorado. That was really exciting because they handed me a check for $100. I was now a paid speaker!

One summer, I was at the United Ostomy Association (UOA) conference in San Francisco. I had meeting after meeting about planning for future conferences. At the same time, an International Ostomy Association (IOA) was being formed. I was invited to go to Malmo, Sweden, the following year for the founding of IOA. I was so excited that I signed up for a course in Swedish. It was just something else to do in my spare time.

In May 1974, my daughter Cheryl turned 15. I decided to take her with me on the trip to the IOA Conference in Europe. She wouldn't be attending the conference. Rather she would be experiencing Europe for the first time and meeting our good friends the Dreckmanns in Hamburg, Germany. She would stay with them when I headed to Malmo, Sweden for the IOA conference. Cheryl enjoyed getting riding lessons offered at Peter Dreckmann's riding school and stables with 55 horses.

There were 13 countries represented at the conference in Malmo. One of the key things that had to be done was to create the by-laws for the International Ostomy Association. When complete, each representative took the by-laws back to his or her country for acceptance. Finally, at the national conference in Denver in August 1974, they would be formally accepted. And I was nominated to be the recording secretary.

We went over the by-laws for IOA. When our time ran out at 6 p.m., we had just gotten to the most important part: the amount of dues each country should pay and how many votes each should have. It was suggested by the chairman that this business be left until the meeting in Denver to finish up. I couldn't believe my ears. I stood up and made a speech that we had all spent so much money to come to this meeting and the purpose of this meeting was to make these decisions. And I thought we should keep on with our business even though it meant we would have to miss some of our fun activities the next day. Everyone agreed and so I was put on a committee of three to meet and present proposals to the group first thing the next morning. Gratefully, the proposals were accepted which simplified the process.

One of the Malmo attendees was a doctor from Greece who was excited and impressed with the work that we were doing. He revealed that there were no ostomy groups in Greece but he would work on setting up a national association.

One of the goals of IOA was to get ostomy groups in countries where there were no groups. We learned of an American ostomate who went to Poland to visit family several years prior to Malmo. He had taken publications on ostomies and several kinds of appliances with him. He talked to a surgeon there who did ostomy surgeries and the surgeon told him, "I do a lot of surgeries and I do good surgeries, but most of my patients die afterward. They don't die from the surgery. They die from depression because I don't know how to tell them how to live with an ostomy. And they don't know. So, they just die."

They needed an ostomy group in Poland. It became one of our goals.

There were eight of us from the US who attended the conference and we hung out together in our free time. I remember a lunch where each of us ordered different things so we could sample lots of Swedish food. When we finished, Don Binder from our UOA home office took each of our monies to go pay the bill. He came back with a handful of bills for our change. After he had parceled out the bills, he placed his bills down in front of him and announced, "And I'll take Park Place and Broadway!" We shrieked with laughter! One of Don's favorite sayings was "Get a stoma and see the world!"

After lunch, we headed to the beach. One young lady with a great figure wore her bikini even though her stoma was placed above her bikini line. She had made a zebra patterned cloth pocket to cover her pouch. One stranger asked, "What's that?" She answered, "Oh, that's where I keep my money!" He said, "What a great idea!" and walked on.

Madame Simone, a millionaires, took a liking to me at the IOA conference. She invited me to her chateau just north of Paris for a three-day visit. Madame's chauffeur picked Cheryl and me up from our hotel and took us to her chateau. I was very curious. As far as I knew, she hadn't asked anyone else from our group.

Well, it was magnificent: a huge three-story mansion on many acres of sculptured lawn with peacocks strolling around. Cheryl and I were given five rooms on the second floor. While looking around my bathroom with all the gold fixtures and trying to figure out what everything was, I pushed the wrong button and pretty soon a maid popped her head in the door and asked what I wanted! At meals, another maid served everything on our plates and as we had to have a clean plate for each course, we often went through five plates in a meal. Madame took us to the opera in Versailles one night and one afternoon the chauffeur took us into Paris and showed us around.

Madame didn't speak a word of English, and I didn't speak any French. There were two German guests there who spoke both English and French, so we got along. Our conversations were really interesting!

After the conference was over, I returned to Hamburg and the Dreckmanns. Cheryl had had a good time while I was gone and we stayed for several more days. It was interesting how formal they were with others, always using the formal form of addressing each other. For instance, Peter's best friend was Dieter Thiele and Peter always called him Herr Thiele and vice versa. I asked Peter if he was insulted when I called him Peter. He replied, "Of course not, you are like family."

Cheryl and I called Wolfgang Kune who had been our exchange student in White Bear Lake. We planned to get together the next day. When Wolfgang picked us up at Peter's, he was wearing faded jeans, a plaid shirt, scarf around his neck, an old leather jacket, and his hair was long. He was exactly the opposite side of society from Peter and the two of them fairly bristled when they saw each other, especially when Wolfgang and I threw our arms around each other in greeting. Peter just stood there and glowered at this display of affection, probably because he and I had only shaken hands the entire time I'd been there.

Wolfgang was just the same, talking a mile a minute. I told him all about Peter and then he told *me* about Peter. After that I saw Peter from a different point of view. Peter was enormously wealthy and Wolfgang was a struggling student living life to its limits and having an incredibly exciting life. When he took us back to Peter's, I showed him around, including our suite of rooms. He pointed out that there were things sitting around worth thousands of dollars.

One evening at the Dreckmanns we watched a movie on TV. Can you imagine how funny it was to hear John Wayne and the Indians speaking German?

After saying our goodbyes, we headed west to Holland where we spent a week with Joan Schwencke and family. What a wonderful, relaxing time, even though we were on the move, seeing wonderful places every day.

Next was planning for two of the biggest events of my life and they were both happening the same week, which I concluded was the dumbest thing I had ever done. First of all, the UOA conference was at the Hilton Hotel in Denver that was connected by a bridge to May D&F, Denver's largest department store, in 1974.

What was I thinking? I had a pottery show there the same week as my UOA conference. Dummy! Second of all, May D&F ordered $8,000 worth of pots for a two-week show for three of their stores. My employees would be demonstrating on the wheel in all stores for three hours each day.

I was one person wanting to be in two places at the same time. Did I survive? Yes. Did both go well? Yes again. Was I exhausted? Definitely yes.

After three years of planning, the UOA Conference I hosted was the best that had ever been held! More than 1,000 people attended. The evaluations rolled in reiterating the same thing: "most organized," "best program ever." And we had the biggest net profit —around $18,000—with vendors showing the latest in ostomy equipment and so much more. I received nothing but superlatives from everyone.

> One of the members of the audience asked him a question about sex.

Even Lynn got into it. We had a panel of ostomate spouses. One of the members of the audience asked him a question about sex.

His answer: "When I'm interested in sex, I'm sure as hell not going to let a bag get in my way!" It brought down the house!

At the final banquet, I was on Cloud 9. The week was over, and I had made fantastic new friends and had been elected secretary to the new International Ostomy Association. April in Amsterdam was in my sights for next year.

Youth Rally

Being so active in the Ostomy Association brought awareness of all young people who were struggling with an ostomy. They had issues that centered around being different from their classmates, about managing an ostomy by themselves instead of having their mother take care of it all the time, about being involved with class activities, and much more. Some had an ostomy because they had spina bifida and had to spend their lives in wheelchairs. My heart went out to them. I had the idea that we ought to create a program just for them: The youth who were dealing with ostomies.

I proposed to the UOA Board that we should do something to help these kids. My proposal included a national Youth Rally for a week on a college campus that had facilities to host something like this. The Board gave their enthusiastic approval of my proposal, gave me a small budget, and told me to run with it! Of course, I chose the University of Colorado right here in Boulder.

When I contacted the University, they were very willing for us to use a dorm, which was empty during the summer. I contacted Enterostomal therapists to come as counselors and they enthusiastically agreed even though they would receive no pay, but their expenses would be covered. Enterostomal therapists, commonly known as ETs, are nurses who have been trained in the care of ostomy patients.

The first Youth Rally with sixty kids in attendance was held in 1978 and has continued to increase in size every year since. We took them into the mountains, had classes on managing their ostomy, and held a party on the patio with a DJ providing the music while they danced. You should have seen the kids in wheelchairs as they performed wheelies!

They loved every minute of it. And our coup de grace was arranging for Rolf Benirschke, the football player for the San Diego Chargers with an ileostomy, to visit and talk to them. His book *Alive and Kicking* is a must read. The kids *loved* him!

Some of their comments that came in afterwards …

I never realized there were other kids like me.

Now I can take care of myself. My mother doesn't always have to do it for me.

I learned about better appliances, how to dress better, and that I am a normal person.

We adults often found it hard to hold back the tears at times. We felt we had given sixty kids a new lease on life. It felt wonderful!

And a comment from attendee Cody Mitchem:

I had no idea what to expect when I flew from Hawaii to San Diego to attend my first Youth Rally. Would I like it? Would they like me?

Four years later, the friends I have made at Rally have become a second family to me. Each year the Rally has been a fun adventure, but also an important part of me learning about my illness and how to take care of myself. This second family has become a vital part of my support system that I know I can always turn to when I need a lift. Did I mention how much fun it is? Every year I look forward to getting together with the friends I've made at the Youth Rally and just being me ... not the sick kid, or the tired kid, but me. And the same goes for everyone else who attends. This is a place where we can relax and enjoy life with others just like ourselves.

My life in general was good. One day I said to a long-time friend of mine that I was feeling lucky. She responded, "*You* feel *lucky*? With all that you've been through? Are you out of your mind?"

As horrible as most people would think it would be to have an ostomy, I credit it with a turning point in my life, which included great adventures, speaking so often that I lost all fear of speaking, and becoming the incident that finally brought back my confidence in myself.

> I was lucky.

And I did feel that way. I was lucky. I had experienced so much, and traveled, and met so many interesting people, and yes, I felt I had made a difference in many lives. I had had an enriched life. I was happy. Few people could say the same.

9
Pottery

Carol Ann Pottery, Ltd., was born!

While we lived in Minnesota at White Bear Lake, I started taking pottery lessons. I loved it! So, when we moved to Boulder, I found classes given by the city of Boulder at the old fire station on the Hill, as the locals called the area. My instructor was Betty Woodman, an internationally known potter. Eventually her work lined the railing at Denver International Airport at one time and was shown at many museums internationally.

My hands, my imagination, and my eyes were opened when I discovered the Boulder Potters' Guild and joined it. The guild was the recipient of my first works in its kiln. My passion for the art of pottery grew, turning one of our unfinished basement rooms into my workshop. When I had several pieces ready, I'd take my pots downtown and fire them at the guild.

I remember one time when at the guild loading the kiln with my pots, it was drizzling rain, my hair was a mess, and my ratty coat was covered with soot and while waiting for the firing, I went to a nearby small grocery store to buy a snack. The looks I got! It was like I wasn't good enough to be there. What that experience did was to make me aware of how people are treated and judged by their initial appearance.

One of my guild colleagues was an accomplished potter in his own right. And Larry Clark also knew how to lay out the foundation for a kiln. It had soon become apparent that I needed my own kiln … and a big one. Coming to my expanding workshop, he had a kiln erected within a week. Eventually, Lynn and I added an addition to the back of the garage, but my success created a "bulging at the seams" problem for my backyard studio. It was just not big enough. I needed to expand "big time."

In December 1974, I bought an industrial piece of property in Boulder and moved my pottery studio out of the house! I talked to the bank about a loan, getting a building permit, lining up plumber and electrician, contractor, fencer that would protect the property, and anyone else that would bring it to life. It was a lot of work and quite exciting. Not surprisingly, many tried to take advantage of me because I was a woman. That didn't last long. They soon found out who they were dealing with! Lynn just laughed every time someone attempted to bamboozle me.

January 1975, the official building began. Two large kilns would be included. The old house on the property would be gutted for new offices, a kitchen, warehousing of finished pots, and shipping. My pottery business was moving to a new home.

Carol Ann Pottery, Ltd., was officially born and ready to handle our growing business! Soon I was turning out nearly 1,000 pots a week! Suddenly, would-be potters asked if they could intern with me.

I started exhibiting at local art shows and then word of my work started to spread. In July 1972, I was asked to exhibit my pots in Rapid City, South Dakota, along with artist Jacquelyn Rochester. Jacquelyn was a well-known artist in the Black Hills even before she moved to Tubac, Arizona. She and I became good

That's going to be a beautiful pot!

friends. In fact, she commissioned me to make 12 place settings of my pottery in return for painting a portrait of Lynn and me in our home in Boulder. Before she died, her paintings were selling for between $6,000 and $10,000. I have two of her originals and my daughter Cheryl has the portrait.

> **Looking like a struggling potter, I was totally accepted.**

Over the next few years, I added more interns. All were unpaid; they came to be taught. I would teach them the refinements of throwing pots and they would do a lot of the "grunt" work in the studio. In the beginning, each would throw 20 cylinders (a straight up vase) and 20 bowls. When finished, I would cut each one open to show them the thicknesses of the bottoms and the walls. They couldn't keep one until I was satisfied.

Soon, they were able to make pots that matched mine, and we would stamp them with the CAW logo. Then we started making

Exhibiting my pottery at an art show

dinnerware. That meant we had to have precise measurements so that people could buy "open stock" pieces that would match in size and color to the ones they already had. They were paid by the piece. If their piece didn't match the measurements, I would smash it and they wouldn't get paid for it. They quickly became excellent potters.

Every so often I would take a week and go on a selling trip. With a carful of samples, I would go east from Denver to Kansas City and come back through Oklahoma and Texas. On these road trips, I would pick up four or five new accounts. When I got back, we would be busy filling the orders.

In between, we would have our own sales locally and we developed a dedicated population who loved Carol Ann Pottery and would bring their friends.

One time I borrowed a beat-up pickup, filled it with pots and headed to Santa Fe, New Mexico. This was my "hippie" phase. One gallery owner invited me to dinner at his commune just north of Santa Fe called Tesuque. The group there consisted of all kinds of artists working in a variety of mediums: jewelry, leather work, stained glass, and woodworking. It was wonderful to see. They lived in small houses scattered around their studios. We ate around a campfire and had a dinner that someone provided if he or she had sold something that day. Looking like a struggling potter, I was totally accepted. I was invited to sleep on someone's couch for the night. It was a wonderful experience.

> My parents are definitely the reason I am what I am.

One thing my business told me was that the people who worked for me all lived on little income. One had been in jail for something; I never knew for what. I had six people throwing pots, two kiln loaders and a manager. I tried to give them bonuses when I could. Now in my hippie phase, I do believe I was working day to day with real hippies.

Gift shows caught my attention. There were six major cities that held gift shows once a year for the buyers of retail merchandise. It was a major ordeal to pack and ship enough pots to set up a display. Totally different from my art shows, now I needed help. Gift shows were demanding in many ways, often lasting four days. Standing for four days can be grueling, giving a sales pitch and, of course, nonstop smiling. Usually, I took someone with me to help, plus being able to relieve each other. The shows were always successful. The bonus was that I made many new friends. And the same people would go from show to show to exhibit their wares.

One time, Mom and Dad came for Thanksgiving. They joined me at the studio while I was getting a large order glazed and into the kiln. While they were waiting for me to finish up, they found things to do. Mom grabbed the big push broom and started sweeping the studio floor, and Dad started scrubbing the sink in the bathroom. The next workday someone yelled, "Wow, Carol Ann cleaned the bathroom!"

"No, my dad cleaned the bathroom."

"Someone cleaned the floor."

"My mom swept the floor."

They all stopped and looked at me. "Your MOM swept the floor and your DAD cleaned the bathroom?"

Yes, yes they did. It was who they were. When they were in their 60s and told me that they were heading to South America for a year to build a church in Argentina, I wasn't surprised. Both were always there with a helping hand … caring for others. Mom was always willing to try new things and experience new adventures. When Mom decided she should learn how to tap dance and drive a car in that decade of her life, I wasn't surprised.

I thought a lot about my staff's reaction to their actions and realized that I hadn't thought about it at the time. My parents are definitely the reason I am who I am. They influenced my attitudes toward people and the fact that I don't get hung up on what sex a person is in relationship to his or her job.

As much as I loved the pottery business and making beautiful pieces, there were many frustrations at times. The potters were always complaining about something or there were issues: the guy who ran the kilns misfired a whole firing, a $1,000 worth of pots lost; the potters weren't paying attention to the sample pieces they were to follow so the pieces had to be trashed; the employees were fighting among each other. Was it because they were all hippies? I don't know.

One day, I gathered them together and shared what my expectations were of them as my employees. I explained that I had thought long and hard about my message. This is what I said:

> Some of you may feel that no matter how well you do, that I keep expecting more of you. Well, yes I do. And I will continue to expect you all to do better and to do more and after you accomplish that, I will expect even more of you. I think anytime we find a way to improve the quality of our product, it should be done. If it takes five seconds longer per pot, so be it for quality!

You are all throwing about twice as fast as you were a year ago. Most of you are earning well over what you expected. Do you hear me complaining? No, I'm delighted. But in return, I ask for more quality and I will continue to expect quality from you. You are getting something in return, in case you forgot. You are being paid more than the minimum wage. You are now getting paid vacations. You are getting a health insurance program. You are getting increasingly better working conditions, and there are other things in the works for the future.

You see, my whole life has been based on constantly pushing myself to do better and to do more. I know it's possible and I get the greatest possible satisfaction out of leading a life like this. The personal rewards are impossible to count.

And so, it should come as no surprise that my company is built like this. And so yes, I will continue to always expect more. That's what this company is all about.

And if that's the kind of person you are, I want you to work and grow with me. If you are not interested in growth development, perhaps you don't belong here, and it's time to leave.

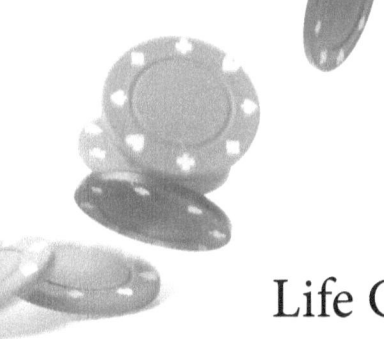

10
Life Goes On

Mom, this was the best gift you could have ever given me.

By now, my kids were in their teens. Pottery had become my new passion, but I never left the ostomy community behind. The building of the pottery business was a major undertaking. At the same time, I was actively supporting ostomy-related events with meetings, speaking, and advising medical professionals on how to work with and enlighten ostomy patients. I would travel when needed.

On January 1, 1975, my calendar for the year (and I hadn't even started filling it in with other stuff!) already looked like this:

Jan 3-8 Lynn and I go to Aspen. He'll ski; I'll sleep!

Feb 5-7 Salt Lake City to open new pottery outlets.

Feb 12-24 A friend from Europe comes to spend 2 weeks.

Feb 27-Mar 2 Phoenix for UOA regional meeting and to open pottery outlets.

Mar 3-5 Los Angeles for national gift show and to pick up new outlets.

Mar 25-27 Dallas for UOA board meeting and to pick up new outlets.

April 24-26 Amsterdam for IOA conference. Take Scott with me.

Aug 20-23 Toronto UOA National Conference.

Aug 23-25 Denver Gift Show.

In April, Scott was 15 and looked forward to his first venture to Europe, and I would attend my IOA meeting in Amsterdam. We started in London and were able to tour for a day or two, then on to Hamburg, Germany, to stay with the Dreckmanns for a week. Amsterdam was next. The exchange student who lived with our family years ago picked us up when we arrived in Holland. Joan Schwencke had invited us to stay with her. While I attended my meetings, she made sure that Scott saw a great deal of Holland.

My IOA meetings were exciting. We drew up the formal version of the Constitution and By-Laws. I was re-elected recording secretary so I'd have to go back to Europe the next year. Tough luck, huh?

My time at the conference ended and now it was time for Scott to see more of Europe. We flew back to London and spent a week touring western England. A highlight for me was spending time with the most famous potter in the world, Bernard Leach, and visiting his studio. He was 88 years old and didn't typically accept visitors. But with the efforts of my English host, we were able to spend an hour and a half with him. My skin actually tingled at times. I felt I was in the presence of greatness. At the end of our talk he said, "The most important things in life are to be happy, to understand, and to do something worthwhile." That phrase made a great impact on me and became the cornerstone of my talks to ostomy groups.

Our final week was on the island of Menorca, near the island of Majorca in the Mediterranean Sea. Before we had left home, I told Scott I would be giving him absolute freedom on this trip.

That is something that most parents wouldn't give, especially to a teenager who was constantly in trouble. He hadn't had that freedom at home. I wanted him to face situations on his own and get himself out of any predicament if he created it. He handled himself extremely well. I allowed him to wander around Hamburg on his own while I was at a meeting. Our hosts were horrified! They said he would never find his way back. But he did. While on Menorca, he went exploring among the rocks on the seacoast. And our host there was also horrified. "Those rocks are razor sharp. The coastline is miles long. If he gets hurt, how would we find him?" But Scott came back after a few hours, excited about his solo adventure.

"Mom, this was the best gift you could have ever given me." 1976 was significant with my gift show presence.

February – Dallas Gift Show

March – Albuquerque Gift Show

June – Las Vegas Gift Show

July – Dallas Gift Show

October – IOA Conference in London

Once again, I took off three weeks to attend the IOA Conference and to tour Europe, but this time without a child. I had become friends with Dr. Schellerer at the IOA Conference. He invited me to watch surgeries at his clinic in Erlangen, Germany. This was not from above looking down through glass but standing right next to the patient and the surgical team. I watched a pancreas resection, open heart surgery, the closing up of brain surgery, and knee surgery. Before entering the surgical floor, I changed my clothes to hospital garb, covered my head, put on mask, and wore special shoes. Still,

I was amazed that I was able to wander about and be so close to the actual surgery. I did wonder about the lack of sterile atmospheres. Something I wouldn't expect would happen so casually today.

My personal life was changing and Lynn and I had grown apart. Separating, I moved into an apartment. Eventually, we divorced but remained friends, which made everything more comfortable. During this time, I received a lot of criticism. Comments like, "You pay too much attention to your business!" Well, you know what? How about the husbands who spend all their time at their office? Those who go on business trips all the time? But when a woman does the same thing, she is a pariah?

My focus was on building the pottery business. I continued to go on marketing trips to pick up new accounts, and soon I bought my own house.

> **I realized that they were actually stunned.**

Even though my business was located in Boulder, I hadn't been active in the business community directly. That changed when I joined the Boulder Chamber of Commerce. Soon I was elected to the Board of Directors and that was one of the most interesting experiences I've ever had. I recall one discussion about something that needed a decision. I sat there thinking that they really hadn't considered one important item so I asked about it. Thinking back, I realized that they were actually stunned. Their token woman had asked an important question. Actually, I believe the members recognized that I could be an asset and treated me well after that. In fact, two years later, I was elected Chair of the Board–the first woman Chair!

President Carter created The White House Conference on Small Business. Its purpose was to learn small business wants and do it through meetings that were held throughout the country.

There would be several hundred people at the Colorado meeting to elect the delegates who would be attending the final meeting in Washington. I wanted to go to the Colorado meeting and be selected as one of the delegates. The head of the Boulder Chamber told me to be sure to ask a question or two when I was there. He said the purpose was to call attention to myself and my intelligence. After all, how would someone get elected out of a group of several hundred people if no one knew who you were? Several were elected to attend the conference in Washington and I was one of them!

The White House Conference on Small Business was held in January 1980. It was absolutely terrific. President Carter addressed the opening and impressed all of us. He is the first President ever to pay attention to small businesses and try to help them. We met in our sessions for four days and started out with about 230 changes we wanted made. Next, we narrowed that down to 60 and then prioritized the top 15. We did some good work.

When I got back, my daughter Marie, now 15 years old, and I left for our trip to Europe. This time, the IOA Conference would be in Milan. Did you notice that each of my children was that age when they went to Europe with me? It was pure coincidence but interesting.

We bought Eurail passes for $220 each, giving us unlimited miles on the trains for three weeks. We probably got our money's worth after just four days! We had no agenda. Everywhere was our destination, which allowed us to change our minds several times a day. What fun we had! We journeyed down the Rhine, saw Neuschwanstein, went to Italy and rode a gondola in Venice. We visited every one of Ludwig's castles, then went to Milan for my five day meeting. Afterward,

> **How do you keep going like this?**

we went to Holland for a few days, where Joan Schwencke was once again a wonderful hostess.

After we returned home, Marie and I left for the Gift Show in Atlantic City. She was wonderful help and a welcomed addition to my "sales" team. She had a little bit of a hard time keeping up with my pace in Europe and after we got home, she asked, "Is this what your life is really like? How do you keep going like this?"

Events and travel in 1980 expanded my work for both ostomy and pottery.

January – Atlantic City Gift Show

February – Chicago Gift Show

February – Anaheim: UOA Board Meeting

March – New York Gift Show

March – Albuquerque: Keynote Speech for UOA meeting

March – Atlanta: UOA meeting

April – Phoenix: UOA meeting

April – Lincoln, NE: UOA Meeting

April – Mexico vacation

June – Rapid City, SD: 25 year high school reunion

July – New York Gift Show with Marie

July – Washington, DC: UOA National Conference

August – Chicago Gift Show with Marie

September – San Francisco: Fun trip

October – Kansas City, KS: Throwing pots for exhibit at Halls Plaza

My work as the chair of the Boulder Chamber of Commerce also kept me busy with meetings and receptions. I enjoyed it greatly. The executive director resigned to take a position in another state. Executive Secretary Sherrie Cline and I stepped up to run the Chamber in the midst of a national search for a new executive director. This was a time when I was doing a lot of public speaking in the community and attending at least three to four meetings a week.

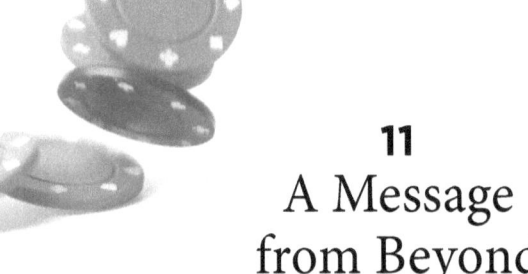

11
A Message from Beyond

They told me that I was to stay and not leave; I had more work to do.

My life was rudely interrupted when I least expected it in the spring of 1981. When sharp pains surfaced, I made an appointment with my doctor. A huge water-filled cyst in my abdomen had been generated from previous scar tissue that needed to be removed. Because of my five major surgeries in the past, doing a minor surgery to rid my abdomen of the adhesions was not something I worried about. This was not to be a difficult surgery, so I was not worried as I entered the hospital. I didn't know that I was entering a six week period of horror.

A few hours after surgery, I started hemorrhaging, resulting in a loss of nine pints of blood. They rushed me back into surgery and took care of the bleeding vessels. For several days, I didn't know if I was alive or not. Instead of getting stronger, I seemed to be getting weaker. Then it became apparent that I had a blockage in my intestine. They watched it very carefully all week and said that if it didn't pass by Saturday, they would have to operate again that day. Everyone except me was told that I had less than a 50% chance of surviving another surgery at that time.

Friday evening, I remember waking up in confusion. My bed was all messed up, my IV tubes were all tangled, the curtains around by bed were all awry, and the air was completely filled with words. I couldn't even see across the room because the air was so filled with words written on paper flying around me. I started pulling the words out of the air and setting them down, and I finally wrote a book using the words surrounding me. Then I went back to sleep. When I woke again, the air was clearer but there were still a few words floating around. So, I picked them out of the air, but this time I wrote a short story.

I slept again and woke to a peaceful, empty, neat room. It seemed to be filled with light. I looked around and there were no lights on, yet there was definitely a warm glow. I enjoyed that warm glow with a sense of utter peace and serenity. And there was no pain. I looked across the room and saw a group of people standing there: I saw Christ, my spiritual guide, my Indian guide, and my grandmother. They told me that I was to stay and not leave; I had more work to do. It had to do with helping women, perhaps in the financial area.

> Well, I can wait till morning.

And soon came the knowledge that I was healed. I knew without a doubt that the blockage had passed and that I was okay. I got out of bed and took my "tree" with me to the bathroom so I could pull out all of the tubes and go home. But I was so weak. I couldn't dislodge a single one. I felt my stomach and again knew that I was okay. I thought, *Well, I can wait till morning.* So, I got back into bed and went to sleep.

> I, my body, my mind, and definitely my spirit had had enough.

The next day when the doctors came, I knew what they were going to say. After examining me, they pronounced that the blockage was gone and that I didn't have to have surgery! I let out a loud YAY! But I wasn't finished with my hospital. I took on hospitalitis. During this time, I was jaundiced and my body illuminated an impressive "yellow all over" appearance.

There's more. While recovering and gaining strength, a stomach ulcer was discovered. For two solid weeks, I had nothing but ice chips. Then, my lungs filled with liquid and had to be drained. Then the worst happened—a fistula! That kept me in the hospital an additional two weeks until I demanded to recuperate at home. My body, my mind, and definitely my spirit had had enough. My children were now adults and on their own, so Mom and Dad came for as long as they were needed. My primary home care instructions were simple: REST!

There were many times friends asked me, "Don't you just want to end it?" My answer, "The thought never even entered my mind. I have too much to do." My guides told me that I was to stay and not leave. They were right!

12
The Next Step

Decisions had to be made:
for the company; for my employees; and for me.

Recovery took several months, and I had lots of support from family and friends. While in the hospital, I depended on my employees at Carol Ann Pottery, Ltd., to keep the business running. My secretary kept me up to date on how the business was doing when she visited me to sign checks. When I was strong enough after returning home, I would show up a few hours a day. At the same time, the country was in a mild recession. I found that this meant the gift market took quite a hit. We really felt that we were slipping behind in a big way.

I hadn't taken a paycheck in a long time. Decisions had to be made ... for the company; for my employees; and for me. It was time to look for another job. Closing Carol Ann Pottery, Ltd., was one of the saddest things I had ever experienced.

In the middle of all this, both of my daughters, Cheryl and Marie, decided to get married ... and within three weeks of each other! I wondered how I would be able to plan two weddings so close to each other when I wasn't completely back to health. But they assured me that they were taking care of everything. And they did.

In the fall of 1982, Cheryl married Cliff Jameson in Denver and Marie married Louis Flores in Tucson.

When Marie married Louis Flores, he was in the Air Force. Within a short time, they were transferred to Torrejon, Spain, which is 20 miles outside of Madrid. I decided it would be a wonderful adventure to go visit them. In 1984, I went over for two weeks in Spain during the Christmas season. The Spanish celebrate Christmas with amazing pomp and circumstance. Many parades and festivities watched over by the Three Kings.

Marie, Louis and I decided to take a trip to Portugal, a beautiful country filled with unusual architecture. It was hard not to buy more than would fit in my suitcase for the return flight.

Flying back to Denver, I had a memorable experience. I was sitting next to a rotund man with a white beard looking somewhat like Burl Ives. During our in-air chats, I found out he was on his way to California; used to live in Estes Park and was a hermit there; now lives in Majorca; travels a lot; is a singer, a folksinger; and would be singing in Denver the next fall with the Denver Philharmonic. *Finally,* I just had to ask, "Please tell me your name." Glenn Yarborough! I also learned that he used to own five lots in downtown Aspen and ran the Limelite Restaurant. And the last time he crossed the ocean was in a boat by himself that took 31 days.

Because of my experience with the Boulder Chamber of Commerce, I knew most of the top players in the Boulder business world. And yes, I was still Chair of the Board. I made a list of the top ten businesses I would like to work for and made an appointment to see the owner of each company. What an experience that was. I had several job offers, all of which I had to turn down because they were not the right fit for what I could physically do at the time. Plus, my passion hadn't been ignited by what they were about.

> My ears and eyes were receptive.

For a short time, I did marketing for an individual who had created a course for the financial planning community, and one that I knew little about at the time. This meant that I was a vendor with a booth at financial planning conferences. My ears and eyes were receptive as I sat in on the presentations and learned a lot. At one of the conferences, I met the main speaker, Venita Van Caspel, and purchased her book, *The Power of Money Dynamics*. One of the financial planners I met at my booth told me if I read Van Caspel's book and still wanted to be a financial planner, then I should go for it!

On the flight home from the conference, her book was the first thing I reached for when I settled into my seat. Not only did I read it but consumed it before the plane landed. I was excited. Was I motivated? Absolutely! At the same time, while I was attending financial conferences and "womaning" a booth, I reconnected with Michael Stein, a member of the Boulder Chamber of Commerce. He was a successful financial planner and talked to me about joining his firm. He knew that my connections with the Chamber would be beneficial. Soon, I joined his firm and started working on my Certified Financial Planner degree (CFP) and my general securities and insurance licenses. In fact, I took three weeks and sequestered myself in my home and studied all day long, every day. They were the hardest courses I ever took! But I passed all the exams and was ready to roll. I was going to be a Certified Financial Planner.

I was with Michael for more than a year and learned a great deal. His leadership style didn't work well for me, so I found another firm in Denver. In 1984, I started working for Alan Gappinger and Arnie Henkel at Century Financial Services. I became one of their star players in a group of about a dozen planners. The next ten years revolutionized much of what was to come in my business career.

Before I go on with my professional life and its profound results, I need to include a factor in my life that was always underlying my decisions, but I just wasn't aware of it. And this factor had a strong impact on my business.

13
Psychic Healing

I tried to explain that it wasn't me that was healing them.

During the same time period that I began working in the financial planning profession, I became interested in psychic phenomena and started taking classes from Barbara Huss, a psychic within the Boulder community who was well-respected. I learned so many things: meditation, chakras, crystals, healing, auras, visualizations, our own spiritual guides, increasing my own psychic abilities, and so much more.

As usual for me, I read countless books on this subject to expand my understanding. As a young adult, I always felt I had some sense of "knowing"—a type of déjà vu. I had a sense that I had been there before, or that I knew ahead what was coming or what was going to be said.

One time I was conferring with an attorney in his office about our mutual client. During our conversation, he told me that before he would enter the courtroom to present his case, he would fill the courtroom with white light and surround the judge with white light. He felt it always led to the successful conclusion of his case. I thought to myself, *Really?!* I then started using this myself. Successful conclusions for my clients became common.

> I often got answers.

I started using white light (a light coming from God) in many different ways. When we would leave to go on a trip, I would visualize, surrounding the house in a bubble of white light to keep it safe until we returned. Then I would surround our car with white light to keep us safe until we returned. During my meditations, I would put out a question to the universe and fill myself with white light.

I often got answers. One time I had been forewarned that I may have to appear in court to testify against a friend. The question I put out to the universe was, *how can I resolve this easily and quickly?* The answer that came: *There will be a peaceful resolution … you won't have to appear in court.* Within ten minutes after I meditated, the phone rang. "The situation has been resolved," the voice said on the other end.

With Mom

One day in my financial planning office, a sudden, incredible stomach pain overwhelmed me. It was so bad, I lay on my office floor hoping it would pass. But it wasn't getting any better, so I canceled my remaining appointments. It felt like the pain I had experienced with my colon cancer. *Is this happening again?* Heading home, I collapsed in bed. A few hours later, Dad called to say that Mom was in the hospital with a tumor on her colon. Surgery was scheduled the next day at 1:00 p.m.

My pain was instantly gone. As soon as we hung up, I called Barbara Huss to share my experience and to ask her if there was anything I could do for my mother. Her response: "Send her white light and visualize her colon as being perfect." Then she added, "Start meditating tomorrow at 1:00 p.m. when she goes into surgery and don't forget the doctors and the nurses. Send them white light, too."

The next day I meditated for about an hour around 1:00 p.m. I visualized Mom in surgery and saw two white forms that seemed to be angels standing right next to the operating table. I was in so much anguish over the pain that I knew she was going through. I asked God to let me take her pain. I found out later that Mom had NO PAIN in the hospital. She did not even have pain shots! I asked God to let me take her pain, and He already had done it!

With Joe

I flew down to be with Mom for a few days. While I was there, Dad told me about his friend Joe Kern who had been repairing something on the roof of the garage when he fell off and smacked his head on the concrete. He also broke his collarbone, broke ribs and collapsed one lung. He had been in a coma for almost two weeks. Returning to my Colorado home in Longmont on January 2, 1984, I meditated and brought an image of Joe into my focus. I wrapped Joe's head with white light. Then, I zapped his head with it. Then I said, *Joe, open your eyes.* I saw that he had opened his eyes, but they seemed vacant. My thoughts to him continued, *Joe, move!* He moved but his eyes still seemed vacant. Later, Dad wrote me a letter that on January 2, Joe came out of his coma but that he had a vacant stare.

Later, Joe lost his vacant stare and recovered.

With my son Scott

I've shared with you that I've journaled and recovered events and my experiences for years. From my journal entry for February 1, 1984, I wrote a passage about my son Scott, 25 at the time:

I was meditating. I seemed to be totally filled with energy—almost paralyzed with it. I decided to use this energy to visit Scott.

I found him standing on a mountaintop in a stance that was filled with energy ... trembling with energy with his limbs wide apart and his head facing upward. He seemed bigger than usual. His eyes were blank orbs with sky-blue and white light like there were light bulbs behind them or he was giving off laser light. The light coming from the eyes was brilliant. I don't know if he was giving off the light or if the light was coming to him.

I became very concerned and asked God to help him, to help him to the best end. I told Scott I loved him. I asked God to let Scott know that I loved him, that I was here, that he could count on me. I said these things and related thoughts many times over.

Then Scott was on the ground, bent over in a tiny crouch, all diminished and wrapped in a little ball. I immediately sent white light to wrap around him and it seemed like a comforter or quilt. In comparison, everything seemed calm, serene and quiet. I hadn't even realized there had been sound before.

And then the energy that had been in me totally drained out and I was left feeling limp.

Later in the month, Scott visited me and brought his journal. His entry paralleled my February 1st entry where I had both sensed and envisioned that he was not in a good place. This is the rest of his story:

> *I was a painter for Steve Householder's company, F&S Painting, in Durango, CO, on February 1st, 1984. It had just stormed that winter day and was too cold and snowy outside to open the bay door, so we were warming up the painter's van inside the maintenance bay with the doors closed. I was mixing paint, sitting on a bucket just a few feet away from the exhaust pipe. Unaware of the fumes I was breathing in, I eventually felt light-headed, saw my vision reduce to a pinpoint, then blacked out.*
>
> *As my awareness revived, I felt myself being manhandled off the floor and carried into the office to be placed in a La-Z-Boy chair. As people spoke to me, I do not recall responding. My eyes were open, and I could see and hear my coworkers but, as if paralyzed, could not respond. I heard that they had called for an ambulance.*
>
> *Sitting in the chair everything became surreal as I experienced thick, dark, shadowy arms and hands come up out of the floor and grab onto my soul from the inside of my body and try to pull me out and down through the floor with them. I was filled with terror, knowing instinctively that this was dying and that they wanted to take me to a very bad place. My terror was deeply intense, as I was paralyzed, powerless to resist.*

> That is when I heard a quiet, sweet, loving voice behind and above me saying, "Why don't you call my name?"
>
> I knew instantly who it was. But I was still paralyzed and couldn't move, so I thought in my mind, "Help me, Jesus!" Nothing happened. The dark evil arms kept tugging on me. I struggled and fought to get my voice out of my mouth to speak His name. It seemed like I fought for several minutes till finally the weak words passed my lips, "Jesus, help me!"
>
> Instantly, the thick, dark, and shadowy arms sunk back into the ground, evaporating and releasing me. I felt myself flooded with a Light and a Joy. Then with the certainty that I would be okay, I received some movement back in my body so that I could move around ... but just barely.
>
> An ambulance took me to a hospital and my blood was tested. The doctor compared the results with the amount of time that had passed and said the carbon monoxide in my bloodstream, at the time of the incident, was well over 60%, which is the fatality level.

Scott could have died. The protection from Jesus, the white light, and his mom wouldn't let that happen.

With my colleague, Alan

For days, my colleague and friend Alan was in terrible pain from a knee injury the previous week. Not wanting anyone to be in pain, I decided to do a healing meditation the evening of April 22, 1985. As I envisioned his torn muscles, I put them back in place with white light, seeing them fully healed. I then packed them with a gold light, followed with the laying of bandages of gold light around the entire leg. Finally, I saw Jesus with him. I knew that he was being healed.

As the evening set in, Alan had a high fever of 103 degrees, finally breaking in the middle of the night. In the morning, Alan's pain was significantly reduced and he could walk. The next week, all pain was gone and he was walking without a limp.

With my Aunt Ethel

My father called to let me know that my Aunt Ethel in Nebraska was admitted to the hospital for surgery to fix a hiatal hernia the following day. Knowing that I couldn't be there physically to offer her support, I decided to come in through another door.

I envisioned Aunt Ethel lying on the hospital bed. I visualized going inside her body to fix the hiatal hernia. While there, I packed the diverticulitis with white putty. Jesus was there as well. But instead of standing next to her like I usually saw Him when I meditated, He sat down beside her and took her in His arms, holding her. When the doctor examined her before her surgery, her conditioned had changed. Surgery was not needed and she was sent home.

With my father

My father was diagnosed with glaucoma. In the meditation I did each morning around this, I saw Jesus lay His hand on Dad's eyes. I then went into his eyeball, cleaned out passageways, kneaded his eyeball, sprayed white light, painted the passageway with white light, and sent pulsating gold light.

When Dad went to pick up his new eyeglasses that the doctor had prescribed that took into consideration his glaucoma, he found that when he put them on, his vision wasn't clear. One eye blurred. He returned to his doctor, taking the new ones with him and said, "The glasses people must have read the prescription wrong."

The doctor examined him and said, "No, the glasses were correct, but your eye has gotten better!"

With Myself

I was in Rapid City for a wedding celebration and in getting ready, I slammed my knee into the bed's metal frame. I hobbled out to the kitchen to get ice, nearly passing out from the pain. Mom and Marie both saw that my knee looked like a bloody pulp, already turning purple. I held ice on it for ten minutes, visualizing that my cells were being strengthened and revitalized. Within that short time, I had no swelling, no pain, and no limp. All of us enjoyed the ceremony and reception. By the next day, the angry color was gone and looked like a light bruise. By the following week, you couldn't even see it.

In 1989, I felt two lumps in my breast. I was very scared and immediately made an appointment for a mammogram. I started visualizing my breasts perfect and filled with white light. I visualized the two lumps shrinking until they were nothing but a grain of sand. And then I flushed them out of my body and sent them out to the universe. Every morning and every night until my follow-up scan, I started and ended with this visualization. When I went in for the second mammogram, my breast was perfectly clear. There was nothing there!

1991 – I went for another mammogram. The next day the nurse called me and said there was dark spot on the X-ray and I was to go in for a needle biopsy. She said they would do an X-ray again when I came in so they could guide the needle to the spot and take a tissue sample to see if it was malignant. I started to visualize my breasts and could see nothing there so I decided that there was nothing there. I visualized a vaporizer in each breast giving off white light steam. I kept those vaporizers going night and day until I got back to the clinic.

When I got to the clinic, I saw the original X-ray and the dark spot on it. The nurse took another X-ray and went to develop it. She came back in a few minutes and said she needed to take another X-ray and went off to develop it. She came back minutes later and said, "Both X-rays show you are clear. There is nothing there!"

This happened over and over every time I had a mammogram. They would call me in for another X-ray because they had seen a dark spot. I continued each time to visualize my perfect body filled with white light. And I *never* had anything show up the second time!

Carol Ann

Pat started working for me in 1985. I told her that a gold Cross pen was a symbol of success for me and as soon as we earned a certain dollar amount, I was going to buy one. We had a good week very soon after that so I bought myself the coveted pen. That summer, when Marie came for a reunion, she brought me another one. "I know you've always wanted one, Mom!" The next January, a professional colleague presented me with a desk set that included a gold Cross pen. At our annual company banquet in January 1987, two of us were presented with desk sets with gold Cross pens! I said, "Whoa universe, I have enough! But it was not to be. The next month, one of the representatives from a major mutual funds we worked with added to my gold Cross pen collection.

The above incidents are just a few of the many that I experienced. Soon, people started hearing about me and started calling on me to heal their friends or relatives. I tried to explain that it wasn't me that was healing them: It was God. He was just using me as a channel. Then it became uncomfortable; I was actually frightened. I couldn't explain it.

So, I just stopped.

14
Back to Work … My New Calling

It became apparent that people going through divorce needed the services of a financial planner.

It turned out that I absolutely loved being a financial planner. And I was good at it. From selling total financial plans to listening to my clients' concerns, dreams, and hopes to loving the numbers that would roll out in front of me.

From being totally creative in the pottery line to imagining how their dreams could turn into true reality with the plans that were created and to my natural grasping of the numbers on the spreadsheets, I would make it all happen.

My goal was to offer a plan that would enable the clients to achieve their financial goals. After getting all their financial information, my assistant would input it into the computer and understandable spreadsheets would be produced. It never failed. I could always see immediately where things needed to be changed to advance my clients to achieve their goals.

One year, the national company I worked for offered a special all-expense paid trip to its national convention in Naples, Florida, for its representatives who qualified by the end of the year. I lived in Colorado. Winters can be chilly and Florida sounded great. I wanted to win that trip in the worst way. The only problem was:

It was September and I was not close to qualifying. So, I called on my experiences with meditation and visualization.

I visualized walking on the beach picking up seashells.

I would stick them in my pockets until my pants sagged with the weight.

I felt the sand beneath my feet and how it felt between my toes.

I could smell the sea air.

I continued to do this for weeks. And ... you know what? I reached my sales goal so easily, it was astonishing! And the trip to Naples was magical. For my mind, my body, my soul ... and for my work going forward.

Abundance/Empowerment

Several months later, I attended a seminar that made a big impact on my life. Ski Milburn had been a trusted colleague for decades. Always on the leading edge of innovation, he was promoting his yearlong seminar series on *Abundance*. His premise was that abundance is absolutely unlimited. We just have to put away old concepts that limit our thinking. His philosophy called to me.

The monthly topics included:
- Forgiveness and Giving Thanks
- Earning & Spending
- Saving, Investing and Giving Thanks
- Women and Other Majorities
- Enlightened Entrepreneurship
- Happy Practice
- Time Management

- Confidence and Self-Esteem
- Marketing Yourself

At Ski's seminar I connected with an old friend who had taken the series the year before. He revealed that he had earned an additional $750,000 that year!

Well, I took the seminar and got so much out of it that I told Ski I would like to take it again. However, he said he wasn't going to teach it again as his business was growing fast and he had to focus on it. I pestered him but he wouldn't give in. I then asked if I could teach it. He finally gave permission for me to use his materials and teach his seminar series, but I would have to rename it. I called it *Empowerment.*

> **Forgiveness is an extremely powerful concept.**

I was astounded at how powerful it was. I received notes from participants telling me how their lives were changing and thanking me for bringing this program to them.

As you know, forgiveness is an extremely powerful concept. I need to share what happened with me with the Forgiveness seminar within the *Empowerment series.* The first day I was concentrating on forgiving someone here in Boulder and it occurred to me that I had never forgiven my daughter Cheryl for the conflict we had all those years when I was forcing her to do her leg exercises. Then I realized that Cheryl was easy to forgive. The problem was me: I was the one who was hard to forgive. Here I was working on forgiving myself and I realized that in order to forgive myself, I needed to ask Cheryl to forgive me as well. Reaching for the phone, I asked her if I could take her to lunch the next week.

I started with apologizing, telling her I felt I had done a poor parenting job and regretted it. In all the years that I had forced her to do her exercises, I had had anger inside about all of it: the time it took from my day; putting her in pain; and her ongoing resistance. I resented it all. I recalled all of the doctor visits, the surgeries, the braces, and the exercises. I talked about how sometimes I had been totally unfair to her. I asked for her forgiveness.

Cheryl sat in silence, absorbing my words. After my talking for a long time and finally giving her a chance to say something, she said, "Mom, I don't even remember all of that stuff!" We continued talking for another hour or so. What was amazing to me was that I had been carrying this guilt for 34 years and she hadn't even been aware of it! Finally, she said, "If Amanda (her daughter) needed exercises and wouldn't do them, I would make her do them, too."

I was telling a close friend about my lunch experience with my daughter. He listened closely, and then said,

> When the doctors told you that Cheryl was handicapped … and if you had treated her like a handicapped child the rest of her life, she may well have been a handicapped child. But you refused to accept that she was and worked damn hard at completing her exercises so she could have a chance at being normal. You, Carol Ann, are partly responsible for your daughter being the successful, wonderful woman she is today.

When he told me that, I broke down and cried. The concept that I was a good mom just never entered my mind. I was so obsessed with the guilt of being a bad mom.

One day during lunch with Ski Milburn, I asked, "When I do healing for someone in another city, it is definitely outside of myself. So how can you explain that?"

"If you consider that when God is in each one of us and God is everywhere at one time, you're tied to everyone with your white light. And when you heal someone, you become one with God and with them and you are all in the same network!"

Pondering his words, I replied, "You know, the healing always does seem to work better if I visualize myself within the person's body."

"That's right!"

That conversation jostled my whole being. I was trying to sort it all out and understand the answer. It seems that I truly do have the ability to tune into information for answers that I need.

Ski is a fascinating person. Not only is he the great grandson of John Muir (Muir Woods), but he's also the coinventor of several patents held by the company he founded, VAIREX Corporation. His skills have been invaluable to me over the years.

He never realized that he was different until he grew up. When he was small, he saw his guide all the time and talked to him and could hear him. Ski doesn't see his guide anymore, but he receives information all the time. If he has a problem about the structural stress in a building, he will go into meditation, ask his question and wait for the answer. It works for him all the time.

And it works for me some of the time. I just need to practice it more. I've been told that "it is not necessarily *practice* but *trusting* that makes the difference."

In the early '80s, I started to see an increase in single women clients, many of whom were divorced. As I listened to their stories, they would describe the events leading to their divorce and plead for help in improving their financial situation.

After seeing those female clients, I wondered: *Why didn't they get financial advice before their divorce?* Without exception, in each of their stories, they got the short end of the stick. Rarely did they understand what they had agreed to. *How could this be? Who was advising them? Who was their advocate?*

For instance, one woman wanted to keep the house, even though the monthly payments were more than she could handle so she had to sell it for a loss. Another got the limited partnerships that her husband claimed were excellent investments and he got all the cash assets even though the limited partnerships could not be sold and were illiquid. Another divorced her full colonel husband after 26 year of marriage. The court didn't award her any of his military pension, which was worth half a million dollars during his lifetime. What she did receive was alimony of $250 per month for six years. This was supposed to be compensation for two plus decades of marriage and more than a dozen moves to support his career!

Statistics show there are 1.2 million divorces in the US every year. That means that every year, another 2.4 million people go through divorce! And if the average cost of divorce is $20,000 per couple, it means that Americans are spending $42 billion—yes, that's BILLIONS—on divorce each year! Scary, isn't it? It's also downright outrageous.

> **When marital property is split evenly in the divorce, so many women go into poverty after the divorce.**

My creative juices were flowing. It became apparent that people going through divorce needed the services of a financial planner. I attended a seminar for attorneys and one of the speakers was Lenore Weitzman, sociologist and author of *The Divorce*

Revolution. Her research revealed that in the first 10 years after divorce, the wife was nearly bankrupt while the husband had increased his net worth significantly. Well, this caught my attention! This opened a new door for me, leading to the researching of legal and financial aspects of divorce for women.

Introducing Divorce Plan™ Software

Why do the statistics show that if marital property is split evenly in the divorce, so many women go into poverty after the divorce? In 1986, I developed a spreadsheet software program called Divorce Plan software and it provided the answer. It made all the difference in the world for my expanding client base. And eventually, I was called as an expert witness in court cases.

The software's spreadsheets showed graphically how any settlement offer would affect each party for several years post-divorce. I'll explain. Let's assume that my client was Mary, the wife. She did not work outside the home but raised the three children and kept the household going. The husband, John, earned $100,000 per year that allowed his family to have a nice home and comfortable lifestyle. As the divorce proceedings commenced, John knew he would have to split the assets with Mary. That included half the 401K, half the stock accounts, plus combined alimony and child support of $1,500 per month or $18,000 a year. He figured that would give her plenty of assets to live on including his monthly check.

It was time for the spreadsheets. It was time for a reality check of what was to come … for both John and Mary.

After the divorce, John's income would enable him to continue to increase his assets. On the other hand, Mary had been used to a budget of $5,600 per month, which included paying for all household bills, clothing for the kids, food, educational needs, health, mortgage, cars and any maintenance needs around the house. The $1,500 a month she would get would only cover a fraction of what she needed for the four of them—her and the three kids. She would immediately need to pull money out of her share of the assets to live on. Within 10 years, all cash and investments would be gone.

> This became my mantra: to help couples settle and not fight it out in court.

John was shocked when he saw the graphs. He could find no flaw with the numbers. Now, John didn't hate Mary, he just didn't want to live with her anymore. He was willing now to discuss a more favorable financial arrangement for Mary, the primary caretaker of their children. And Mary embraced the idea of budget counseling for herself.

This became my mantra: to help couples settle and not fight it out in court.

Another wedding! Years later, my son Scott married Evelyn.

Let me tell you a bit about Scott. When he was age 24, he drove up from Durango to spend the weekend with me in Longmont, Colorado. He brought a box containing his handwritten personal journals. He had started journaling when he was age 18. I looked though them and was amazed. After a lifetime of no indication of his thoughts, feelings, or emotions, here were more than two dozen spiral notebooks filled with his life! I said, "Scott, these writings are incredible. Such profound insights and thoughts. Others need to read these. I would like to copy your notebooks, transcribe them and put them in a book. How do you feel about that?" He simply said, "OK."

For years, we worked haphazardly to input the hundreds of pages. Finally in 2020, we finished the book: *My Son's Search for Meaning* by Carol Ann Wilson and Scott Eric Wilson.

Scott was a true hippy when we started the book, living out of his car. When he was age 26, he joined the Navy which shocked us all. It was in the middle of his Navy career when he married Evelyn.

15
A Quantum Leap Is Ahead

The objective was to help provide financial security after divorce.

As a member of the National Speakers Association, we met one Saturday a month to hear from top national speakers on how to improve our speaking skills. At lunch, we would sit at round tables for eight and share our backgrounds with the others. One Saturday, my seatmate was an attorney who shared, "I had a husband who was getting divorced and when I saw the graphs from the wife's expert, I told my client, 'We want to settle and not go to court. I don't want the judge to see these graphs!'" That got the attention of all at the table.

I laughed ... and then revealed that report was mine! All eyes shifted to me.

The '80s delivered a major fact gathering time for me about divorce. I consumed books, attended legal education classes, spoke to and met with lawyers, and got out and away from my desk speaking to hundreds of individuals who had been through divorce.

Quickly, it became evident that something was wrong with the system that divorcing couples go through. It seemed that an equitable settlement could and should be found that would help preserve financial security after divorce for both the husband and the wife. That belief became my theme song and my new direction.

Before long, divorce attorney Barbara Stark entered my life and became a major influence as I worked with women going through divorce. Barbara is the author of *Friendly Divorce Guidebook for Connecticut: creating a commonsense approach to divorce planning and negotiating.* In fact, I probably learned most of my knowledge of the law from listening to Barbara so many times. Together, we developed a seminar series designed for both women and men. The seminar attendees were appreciative that they could attend a three-hour seminar for less than $50 and walk away with hundreds of dollars' worth of information that could save them many thousands in mistakes and legal fees. Topics covered included property division, taxes, pension plans, alimony, child support, legal rights, and the local rules of divorcing. A sample case was always shown that illustrated the dire consequences of not making good financial decisions *before* the divorce was final. Attendees would line up afterward to make an appointment with one of us or sometimes both of us.

My financial practice evolved. I was now working with clients going through divorce who came in almost entirely on a referral basis. Colorado lawyers were hearing about my ability to testify in court as an expert witness. I helped them get more equitable settlements for their clients. Of course, it didn't always work. I appeared in court more than 125 times with my charts and graphs to testify. It usually ended up with a better result for my client.

> **My client came away with an excellent outcome.**

The reports generated from the software showed how different settlements would affect each client for the rest of his or her life. This was useful information for the client, who was having to make decisions; the lawyer arguing the case; and the judge, who could use the information to make a fair decision.

One time, the judge spoke up as the spreadsheets were presented in his courtroom. "Would you please run another scenario by me. I will pay for it myself." I did and my client came away with an excellent outcome.

Expanding My Idea and Concept

In 1986, Quantum Financial, Inc., was formed with the idea of working with people going through divorce to create a financially equitable solution for them. It seemed important to do pre-divorce financial counseling. The objective was to help provide financial security after divorce. This led to teaching other financial professionals how to specialize in divorce planning.

Mediation and Collaborative Divorce

These are two ways of helping clients settle their divorce. In fact, Collaborative Divorce is where both attorneys work with both the husband and the wife. The bottom line is that this erases the terrible arguments and in-fighting as well as making it easier on any children.

In 1989, I told Alan Gappinger, the owner of Century Financial, that I just couldn't work for two companies at the same time. I wanted to see if I could make my own company, Quantum Financial, stand on its own. Requesting a three month sabbatical from Century, I would decide if Quantum would succeed and support me, or if I would be coming back to Century full-time. Alan supported my decision. I would offer my divorce financial planning under Quantum and if there was any investing that needed to be done for clients, I would do it through Century Financial.

Well, succeed it did! Landing on the radar screen of national newspapers and magazines, the interviews generated were countless. I hired an assistant who contacted all the service organizations in the area including the Lions, Jaycees, and Kiwanis groups. Each needed a speaker every week at its meetings and I offered my speaking skills for free. I was swamped with giving talks. After my talks, appointments were made to see me. And because I was so successful in getting them better assets in their settlement, they wanted me to invest their money for them. I was succeeding with Century at the same time!

In 1990, attorney Edwin Schilling came into my life. Ed was a national expert in dividing retirement plans in divorce and drafting QDROS that retirement plans required. His expertise was essential for my clients.

The two of us quickly realized that almost every client and attendee to our presentations asked the same questions. A book collaboration was next on our joint list. We decided to write one that would answer the most commonly asked questions. The *Survival Manual in Divorce* would be created. After consulting with an expert in book publishing, we changed our title. He told us about the lady who wrote a cookbook ... another cookbook! The sales were miserable. But when she changed the title to *Cookbook for the Working Mother,* the sales jumped off the charts! The point being that we had to have a niche. Our new title was *Survival Manual for Women in Divorce*. We had to reprint it five times! This was followed by *Survival Manual for Men in Divorce,* another winner and reprinted four times!

> **The media kept calling me.**

Oh, my gosh! It just occurred to me. I had totally forgotten what the spirits in the hospital had told me: The spirits said that *I was to stay; I had more work to do. It had to do with helping women, perhaps in the financial area.*

And here I was, doing just that!

The media kept calling me. In March 1997, I got a call from New York asking if I could fly out, all expenses paid, to tape a show on *Geraldo*! So, I did. The show was on divorce. They told me the name of another woman who was also coming. Her name was Judith Briles and she lived in San Francisco. I looked her up and called her to connect. She said she was speaking at a women's conference in Denver and we could connect before we headed to New York and appeared on the show together. And Geraldo actually held up my latest book, *Financial Advisor's Guide to Divorce Settlement*, and even read a paragraph from it.

Afterward, Judith told me that she was being interviewed on the *Barry Farber Radio Show* that evening and invited me to come along. Well, after Barry introduced Judith and told all about her, she pointed to me and said, "Barry, the one you really need to interview is Carol Ann Wilson. She is making groundbreaking strides

You can almost see me at the front of the room speaking at a financial forum.

in the area of divorce." So, he did. Imagine! She gave up her time for me! But that's who Judith is. We have been firm friends ever since. It wasn't long before she moved to Denver and then we worked together frequently.

I was asked to speak at financial forums, which led to requests from financial planners to learn how to do the same thing. In 1993, I formed the Institute for Certified Divorce Planners (ICDP) that conferred the designation of Certified Divorce Planner (CDP) to those who successfully completed the program. I remained President of ICDP until December 2001.

Things weren't always rosy. There were some serious bumps in the road at times. Consider this one.

My Institute in Atlanta was the most awful seminar that could possibly have happened. We had the largest group ever in a seriously inadequate meeting space. The expression "packed like sardines" would not be an exaggeration. And the hotel did not have a larger room available. They were contracted out over our dates. In addition to being squished together during the two and a half days, the computers went down seven times! It interrupted learning concentration so badly that everyone was totally frustrated.

Some complained to their home office, some complained to us. We complained to the hotel and to the computer suppliers. It was a nightmare!

More books were to follow. In 1998, Ed and I teamed up with Dr. Judith Briles for *The Dollars and Sense of Divorce*.

With Judith showing our recent book.

The year 2000 brought out my book, *Financial Guide to Divorce Settlement*. And in 2003, another joint venture with Ginita Wall, the *ABCs of Divorce for Women*. And I think my best book of all, *The Ultimate Guide to Surviving Your Divorce,* published in 2014.

In the Meantime …
I was enjoying extracurricular activities.

One of my large financial planning clients lived in Sedona, Arizona. I loved going to see her there as I could also see my daughter Marie. We found out about the four major vortexes in and around Sedona and were determined to visit all of them. We had visited three of them but still were unable to get into Boynton Canyon, a box canyon known to be the most dramatic and beautiful of the four vortexes. Then, someone decided to put a housing development in front of the canyon that closes it off to everyone, and they even put a gate with a guard at the mouth of the canyon.

Well, Sedona is filled with people who are into metaphysics. It just seemed to them to be an abomination, building all these homes and buildings in that area and scraping the land with bulldozers and creating such a fuss and disturbing the Indian spirits. And what is interesting is that it seemed that the big machinery kept quitting and breaking down and the projects couldn't seem to finish on time.

Marie and I were having lunch with my client and she told us how to get in past the gate so we could start hiking back into the canyon. The scenery was indeed dramatic. It seemed we stopped every 10 feet to take a picture during the mile and a half we hiked.

We were in the midst of red rock walls up to a 1,000 feet high all around us with areas scooped out. It reminded me of a couple of things—the Grand Canyon and beautiful Lake Powell—with lots of little areas that could have been caves where Indians had lived. Then there were spires of rock. On the canyon floor it was very green with lots of vegetation plus lots of trees. There was drama everywhere we looked: in the brilliant green below us; the brilliant red rocks around us; and the brilliant blue sky above us. No movie set could recreate nature's impactful presence that we were blessed to be experiencing!

Marie found a place between the rock walls and sang a gospel hymn at full volume, which reverberated as it bounced back and forth between the walls. On our way out, a couple said it was so beautiful that it brought tears to their eyes.

We got to the end of box canyon so we started back. At one point I cut through the brush and across a creek and came upon a meditation circle where I sat for a while and meditated.

I went on my first of many river raft trips. It was unbelievably exciting. I had thought I would be soaking wet the whole time but that wasn't so. Splashing through the white water was exhilarating.

Then I climbed my first fourteener. There are 53 peaks in Colorado over 14,000 feet tall and it's almost a frenzy among many Coloradans to climb as many as possible. So, it seems like a good thing to do once a person turns 50, don't you think? And I'll have to tell you, I huffed and puffed all the way up. The air at that altitude does funny things to you. It makes you think you're having fun even though you're so out of breath and your muscles are so rubbery, you're almost physically sick.

My friend Kamilla Macar and I had been hiking and camping together for years. Then we discovered the Colorado Trail which crosses over the mountains of Colorado while staying in the wilderness. It goes from Denver to Durango and is nearly 500 miles long. We hiked a bit of it and experienced the incredible beauty of the mountains and made the decision to hike the whole trail within the next five years. We would take both cars and place one at each end of the section we wanted to cover that weekend. Then we would camp in between. What a wonderful, relaxing experience.

My son Scott was in San Diego, stationed on an aircraft carrier. I took a four-day vacation and went out to see him, his ship, and to visit my friend Sherrie Cline.

Hiking the Colorado Trail

Sherrie and I talked for hours about how I take risks and why I am that way. She seemed hardly able to believe how I pull myself up by my own bootstraps when a medical emergency surfaces, how persistent I am, how I take risks, and how I keep on keeping on. She always talks about me and what I do with a lot of awe. She asked if my parents took risks. I said no, I didn't think they did.

I then sketched out Mom and Dad's life: Matter and Fraley Engineering; building a church in South America; and investing.

I shared with her about how we played games in the car: guessing games, observation games, and thinking games. How we talked at the dinner table. I described how Dad would bring a puzzle and we kids would puzzle it out and how he would talk to us kids when he was doing something so we could learn every step along the way, constantly teaching us. And then I told her how Mom always took classes and did crafts and was always making things for the house or for people and ways the house was filled with things she made or did. Finally, I told her how Mom would allow us kids to sit around and create our own abominations while she was creating her masterpieces. The result is that we learned about design and beauty and creating and keeping busy.

Sherrie then said, "Of course they took risks! Compare that to my father who worked for the government. He always did what he was told; took vacations when he was told; always worked for someone else; and may never have had an original thought."

My *God*, how lucky and *fortunate* I was. What wealth and richness my parents gave to me. What a sense of living, of creating for myself, of taking charge of my own life. I would hope that I have given even just a part of that to my own children. My parents were not "wealthy," but they gave me riches beyond imagination. Whew … thinking back to what both did in their kaleidoscope of activities was amazing. They created a palette of parenting and guidance that was a masterpiece.

And on top of that, my parents gave me love and security and a sense of self-worth, and the importance of being persistent in order to succeed in the end. The most important fight was learning to be *positive* and believing in myself. The realization that I could do anything I wanted to!

I wonder if people who don't have this ever are able to catch up. Of course, they must. You hear wonderful stories of incredible successes coming from miserable beginnings. So how do they do it? I mused with Sherrie about the fact that my brother and sister are not like me at all and we had the same parents. Does some of it come from a previous lifetime? What about the adversity I've had in my life?

Sherrie finally said, "You *are* your father's child."

16
Love Walks In

I thought about Bill all the time.

Starting in the mid-80s, I belonged to a mastermind group. For more than 15 years, four to six of us would meet each Friday at 7:00 a.m. We discussed issues with our businesses and gave each other ideas and support. Over those 15 years, we got to know one another well. During this time, my colleagues decided that I had been single long enough. I laughed out loud when they proposed that they would write an ad for me for the *Boulder Daily Camera* Personals column. Joining in the fun, I went along with it.

One ... just one person responded. The day after the ad ran, my phone rang. Introducing himself as "Bill," we decided to meet for lunch that week. Neither of us knew the other's last name.

We were having a delightful time telling each other what we did without revealing too much about ourselves. Finally, Bill said, "I know your last name. It's Wilson."

"How do you know that?"

"Well," he said, "I just broke up with a lady who is going through divorce and she was counseled by a lady named Carol Ann Wilson."

Both of us laughed at the coincidence! We were really enjoying each other's company and made plans to go for a walk the next day, then it was a hike, then a dance, then a movie. We couldn't stay away from each other. Quickly, we became inseparable. We wanted to be together every minute.

Bill was like a big teddy bear to me, generating a warm smile to all, and ready to embrace others with his humor and welcoming nature. I learned he used to play football at the University of Colorado.

Hugging Bill

Our first lunch was in September 1993. By November, we decided he should move in with me. Shortly after everyone knew us as a couple, we started making plans to be married the following May. My kids were excited for me. My parents had already met Bill. When we told them of our plans to marry, my 80-year-old Mom asked, "Why are you waiting so long!"

On May 1, 1994, I became Carol Ann Wilson Fullmer.

Our honeymoon was spent in the San Francisco area visiting all the attractions, including Napa Valley and the wine-tasting experience, the Muir Woods, and Hearst Castle. We loved every minute of it.

About the time of our second anniversary, the College for Financial Planning hired me to speak at a financial congress in Hawaii. What a place to hold it and neither of us had been there before! We added a week on to the time I would be there on business and rented a car to explore Oahu, the beaches, and the scenery. Another highlight was going to see entertainer and Hawaiian legend Don Ho. He was so entertaining for his audience of oldsters.

> What a wonderful happening!

We all laughed when he said to us, "I hate that song." Of course, he was referring to *Tiny Bubbles*, his signature song that opened and closed each show. Being the show pleaser he was, we even got a picture of us with him and of me kissing his cheek.

Then we flew to Kauai with the thought of staying at a B&B we had heard about. To our dismay, we learned that the B&B was booked solid. However, the owner was very gracious and offered up an idea. "We're full but I have a cottage down the road that I have up for sale. You can stay there if you like at my regular rate."

What a wonderful happening! It was a modern cottage right on the beach, very private, and with palm trees to shade us when we wanted to sit outside watching the waves. We thought we were in heaven.

We had heard about the Awa Awa Pui Trail that is part of the Waimea Canyon, also known as the Small Grand Canyon. It was a seven mile hike and so beautiful! And what a surprise, because we live in Colorado at a high altitude, being at sea level was a huge advantage in walking and definitely in hiking. Routinely, we swiftly walked past those on trails—locals and visitors alike.

My Speaking World Expands

One day at my office, I got a phone call from Canada with three people on a speaker phone. They were planning a financial congress in each of the seven provinces in Canada. The lead voice on the call asked if I was interested in speaking at each one on *How to Help Your Divorcing Client.*

Well, of course I was interested! They asked about my speaking fee. It's $3,000 per talk plus expenses."

There was a short silence on the line and I thought I had asked for too much. But their first response was, "Well, that sounds reasonable."

Dates were identified and an agreement was put together. Later, I found out that their other speakers asked for much more than I had.

Because of the work that Bill did, he was able to join me for many of the trips and we were able to see a lot of beautiful Canada. One of the other speakers who spoke right after I did was Frank Abagnale, the man who wrote *Catch Me If You Can* that was later turned into a film starring Leonardo DiCaprio. At that time, he was a convicted felon turned author and consultant to law enforcement. He was absolutely fascinating!

Frank Abagnale wowed his audience with his stories

We speakers enjoyed sitting with him behind the scenes listening to his stories. His way of storytelling was woven with laughter. He told us about the latest scam going on at the present time.

It takes place in Grand Central Station in New York where the bad guy would target a successful looking businessman and lift his wallet. Then with the information in the wallet, he would call the home number and speak to the wife, telling her that he had found her husband's wallet and would send it to her immediately. That way, she would not have to go to the trouble of canceling all the credit cards. After spending the cards to the limit, he would just throw away the wallet.

I thought about Bill all the time. I was experiencing unconditional love that I had never experienced before. One of my embarrassing moments was when I was testifying in a divorce case.

The attorneys took a minute to discuss a certain legal point and I found myself daydreaming about Bill while I was on the stand testifying! That shook me up a bit and I never let it happen again.

He joined me in Boston after I had held the training for the Institute for Certified Divorce Planners. Typically, twenty people would be in attendance. A four-day vacation was planned when it ended. We headed to Cape Cod, and then drove to Woods Hole to take the ferry to Martha's Vineyard. Having no reservations, we would have to wait for hours for a place on the ferry. Bill didn't want to. He was ready to turn around and do something different.

Not me, I wanted to see Martha's Vineyard. I convinced him to park, repack into our black bag, and take the ferry as a walk-on. Once there, we could shuttle or walk where we wanted to go. And that's what we did, having a marvelous time. We stayed at Captain Dexter's B&B in Edgartown, walked all over, saw whaling captains' homes, shopped, ferried to Chappaquiddick, picked up shells, and had a delicious dinner. On the way back, Bill told me how things were so different with me. He would never have shifted plans like we did and he was sure glad we did.

> We danced around the house, so excited!

Bill worked for a book and magazine company. He got to meet and have his picture taken with Louis L'Amour. But he wasn't happy with his job and was looking around. We found an ad for a video supply business where he would supply the wall of videos in Mom and Pop stores in a five state area. It came with 10,000 videos and a van reconfigured to be a miniature video store. It seemed perfect for him and we got excited about bidding on it. I liquidated most of my investments for the main payment and the rest would be paid out of earnings. The day we found that our offer was accepted, we danced around the house, so excited! So, on August 4, 1997, Movie Man Enterprises was born.

Bill was excited about his new venture, however the challenges were daunting. Some accounts fell away and it was more difficult than he thought to line up new ones. Movie Man Enterprises was creating stress in our life. It wasn't going together as we had thought. Several accounts canceled, the new ones were small, not enough new ones were started, and expenses were higher than we had planned. But he loved the work and worked very hard at it.

Soon, I was paying off his credit card accounts.

One October, we went with friends on a cruise. We stayed at the Westin in Puerto Rico before the cruise and it was lovely. We swam in the warm ocean and bobbed up and down in the gentle waves. I couldn't stop laughing. Then we hiked in the rain forest in Puerto Rico—wonderful!

December was always an important time for Bill and me. It was the time for our annual retreat to the mountains. Each year, we would review the past and set our goals for the next year. Those times were magical for us. Besides being able to totally relax, we played games, worked puzzles, hiked, and spent a lot of time going over our goals. We talked about them, shared our reasons for them and supported each other in our dreams for a successful year.

First we would list everything we wanted—everything. Sometimes, we had as many as 100 to 150 goals. Typically, we achieved 50 to 60% of them, so if we set more goals, we actually achieved more!

The next step was to divide them between five categories: career, lifestyle, physical, social, and spiritual. Then we would choose one or two from each category that were the *most* important in that category. That would create our list of top ten most important goals for the year. It was amazing to see those goals come true as we focused on them.

For Movie Man Enterprises, Bill wanted to add to his line to increase sales. He planned to attend the Denver Gift Show every year. At one show, he got excited about the display of Dickens Village Department 56 miniatures and took me in to see them. Because I was definitely into hand-thrown pottery, I was lukewarm about these little houses and buildings. But as I looked more closely at their extreme detail, I decided to give them a try. We bought three of them at first and displayed them with our Christmas decorations. Then, we bought more, and then more! Soon, we had quite a display.

Our New House

And in the midst of all of this, Bill and I decided to build a new house in Longmont, Colorado. We were so excited. It had everything I had ever wanted in a house: a neighborhood where the backyard was on a greenbelt; high ceilings and curving staircase; kitchen nook, large working island and fireplace in the kitchen; flowing floor plan that would welcome dozens of people for parties; huge basement that would accommodate Department 56 village and train; and a view of the Rockies ... at least until more homes and trees grew. We moved in the first of the year 2000. The house was almost 4,000 square feet and the house of my dreams.

When we moved into our new house in Longmont, Colorado, we had a 14 x 20 foot room in our lower level that we set aside for the entire Department 56 display. We had help from members of the local Department 56 Club building the mountains, the streets, the railroad tracks, and the ambience. It was really quite a show!

Bill and I were really into Christmas. We used to say that our car had a serious fault. It would come to a dead stop when it passed a Christmas shop! So, with all our decorations and the Department 56 village, our home was soon on the list of Christmas tours. And when people would enter the front door, their jaws would drop open. We looked like a Christmas store. Every surface was covered with unusual Christmas items and dioramas. Even the second level of the house was fully decorated. Then, the piece de resistance, we would take them to the lower level where they would ooh and aah when they saw the village. It was a magical time.

In 2000, the 25th anniversary of the International Ostomy Association was held in Germany. As one of the founders, I was included in the honors. And I looked forward to seeing all my old friends from years earlier. This time, Bill would be with me. We added several days for a vacation and we became tourists for a week. It was his first time to Europe. We rented a car and I became the tour guide, showing him so many places that he had never even heard about.

Barbershoppers

Bill joined the Barbershoppers and really loved it. He became a singer after I met him. A friend had encouraged him to join and Bill immediately knew he needed to get better. Hiring a voice coach for several months, his voice improved and I could hear it in his performances.

The Barbershoppers put on several shows a year for the public as well as competing with other choruses from a three state area: Wyoming, Utah, and Colorado. Regional and state competitions followed. As we traveled to the competitions, our "new family" and friends grew.

Bill with his Barbershop Quartet

Besides being in the chorus, Bill was also in a quartet. The four of them routinely got together just to sing. As time progressed, the quartet changed as stronger voices and skills were added. After years of perfecting his presentation and voice, his quartet was included in the annual show where they were well received by the audience.

It was interesting to me to learn all about this new (to me) venue and what the judges were looking for when they awarded the winners. My ears were now tuned to harmony, choreography, timing, and so much more.

Football

Another event came along that made an impact on our lives. Bill had played football for CU—the University of Colorado—and we had season tickets for the CU Buffs and the Denver Broncos. CU had a program where they paired up freshmen football students with local families. The application that Bill went through was intensive. We would be a type of foster family and Bill would be a mentor to each player that came under his wing.

The first freshman football student we had was Tyler Brayton, a 6'5", 240 pound young man who was a delight to know, and we welcomed him into our home. Years later, I received a letter form Tyler thanking us, and Bill for the guidance that he had given to Tyler when he first arrived in Colorado. The next year, we received Nick Clement, another wonderful football player. We had these two young men at our family functions and everyone loved them.

Tyler went on to become a professional player, first with the Raiders, then with the Carolina Panthers. We were thrilled to keep in touch, watch their growth and success, and celebrated as they got married and had children.

Tyler Brayton towered over Bill and me

We belonged to a Diner's Club where the host each month would put together a menu. Then the others would sign up for something to bring from the menu. Our house was the only one that could seat all the members at one table. We typically would have 20-22 people at each event. When it was our turn to host the event, we would stretch our dining table into the living room and everyone could see each other. At the other homes, we would be separated into two or even three tables.

For some reason, our dinner group got into discussing the Personals column in the daily newspaper. And an older male member, one who always had strong opinions, piped up forcefully saying, "Anyone who has to advertise for a companion is a *loser*. They are all LOSERS!" Bill and I looked at each other and smiled.

We never told anyone how we met. When asked, we would always reply, "A good friend set us up on a blind date."

A Day Never to Be Forgotten ... September 11, 2001

I was in Salt Lake City, Utah. I had spoken at a financial planning conference the day before. I got up early, packed my suitcase and headed down in the elevator to go to the airport to return home. A lady in the elevator looked at me and asked, "Where are you going?"

"To Denver."

"How are you getting there?"

"I'm flying."

"Well, haven't you heard? America is under attack! They are bombing everywhere! All airplanes are grounded!"

We reached the first floor and she ran off the elevator. I got out and just stood there, staring at the opposite wall. *What? What did she say? Huh?*

I got back on the elevator, went back to my room, turned on the TV, and sat mesmerized as I watched what was happening.

I called Bill. Hearing my voice, he immediately said, "I will be there tonight. We will drive home together."

I called the front desk of the hotel and told them I was staying an extra night and would check out the next day. It was the last day of the conference. I decided to return to the exhibit hall where vendors had booths set up. The hotel had brought in large TVs so we could watch. I saw one vendor packing up his booth. He looked like a zombie. He had just watched the North Tower collapse and along with it, his whole company and all of his friends. I stayed in the hall for several hours, just being with everyone.

Eventually, I returned to my room, glued to the TV. What was unfolding was truly unbelievable. Bill arrived approximately eight hours after I had heard his words, "I'll be there tonight." I can't remember how many times we just hugged each other. Returning home the next afternoon, we were both grateful to be there.

In six weeks, I was scheduled to speak at a Morgan Stanley conference in New York. I tried to reach my contact person, Phyllis, who worked somewhere on the 44th through the 74th floors of the South Tower. For weeks, I tried to reach her and I was really worried. Finally, I did get her on the phone. "Phyllis, I've been so worried about you. Tell me what happened with you."

"Well, I was late getting to work that day. And as I was coming up out of the subway, I just saw bodies falling to the ground right in front of me!"

She shared that only six lives were lost of Morgan Stanley's 2,700 employees. I didn't understand how that could be possible. I had watched the South Tower collapse. I asked, "How is that possible?"

"Remember when the Trade Center was bombed a couple of years ago? We put into place evacuation procedures that we practiced from time to time. Our offices were in South Tower. When the North Tower was hit, everyone immediately followed the evacuation procedures. We started down the stairs. Then the announcement came over the building loudspeakers, urging everyone to stay put. We heard, 'Please do not leave the building. This area is secure.' But we had our procedures and ignored the announcement. We kept going down the stairs. So, the end result was that we only lost six of our 2,700 employees"

As she told me this, I choked up with tears.

17
Storm Clouds Ahead

How could I not see the handwriting on the wall?

Things were looking rosy for me. The Institute for Certified Divorce Planners, the ICDP, was taking off. Memberships increased and participants were signing up for trainings and were excited about what they were learning to help their clients. An extensive workbook had been created and experts in their field were brought in to help teach the material within each training session. They included Barbara Stark, a well-known attorney who was skilled in teaching attorneys on how to try court cases; Ed Schilling, a national expert in the field of dividing pensions and drafting QDROs; CDP Carolyn Madden, a successful financial planner; and CDP Linda Leitz, another successful financial planner.

We scheduled several four-day live certification seminars per year in large cities around the US. Each was fully attended and the buzz had started about the trainings that the Institute was offering. When completed, a participant would become a Certified Divorce Planner. An Advanced Institute was added along with a Marketing Institute that would support participants in helping to make the public aware of who and what they could do.

> **Little did I know that the *real stress* was just about to start.**

The four of us ladies would travel together to teach the seminars and we became quite close. I would take them out to dinner at a fine restaurant and our laughter would resound throughout the dining area.

With all I was doing, headaches surfaced. I assumed that they were fueled by stress that the added workload created from the needs of the Institute, along with the travel, being a meeting planner and the building of a new company. Little did I know that the *real stress* was just about to start.

In early 1998, my team was in Miami for our four-day Institute seminar. Jason and Doug, financial planners with a large financial planning firm in Texas, attended our class and paid very close attention to everything. Throughout the four days, there is a lot of time for socializing. Carolyn Madden was my second in command, filling in for me when I couldn't. She came to me to tell me that the gentlemen were not just participants. They appeared to be gathering information, and they told her they were intending to take over the company ... *my company.*

And sure enough, a short time later I got an offer from the owner of the Texas company, a Mr. Browne, to buy my company.

With Ed's guidance, we copyrighted and trademarked my material and software before the meeting with Browne. We knew that we had something unique and would be a benefit to the financial planning community. In May 1998, a meeting was set up with Mr. Browne and me in Dallas after our Institute had completed its final session there. I was trying to determine what I wanted before I met with him. *Did I want to sell what I had just created?*

Over a six hour meeting with Browne in Dallas, he made it clear that his company had the financial resources and network to grow the Institute exponentially. He offered $375,000. His idea was to structure "the sale" in the form of a loan for tax purposes with me staying on to run it at $90,000 per year plus back end bonuses.

The back end was the risk. Bonuses weren't specified as to amounts. It was simply unclear. I would be speaking, developing product, and promoting the Institute. Promotion is easy for me, but I was uncomfortable promoting Browne's company as part of it. One of his goals in obtaining the Institute was to expand his company by having the top CDPs as part of it.

> I was already feeling relieved at the thought of not having to struggle.

I thought if I could get clarity on what my role would be; that I wouldn't be promoting Browne; and that I could get decent front end and back end moneys; I would be okay with it. I was already feeling relieved at the thought of not having to struggle with promoting and setting up all of the Institutes.

During the meeting, a bad headache landed. Reaching for pain pills as we spoke, I continued to listen. We did it! We put together a deal! It felt good to me even though it sounded strange to others. There was a real feeling of security about it. The contract was signed in 1998, a contract I would later regret.

After the sale was completed, Browne sent Jason to act as a supervisor as the Institute was brought in under Browne's umbrella. Jason would look over everything we did and make changes. Within a short period of time, he undermined my way of running the Institute. Everything that I had done to build camaraderie with the graduates and each new Institute was trashed.

Within a few months, tensions grew. My stress increased, along with the headaches. Bronchitis plagued me that was fed with steroids, antibiotics and "happy medicine."

During this time, Carolyn Madden was killed piloting a small plane when it crashed in the mountains. It really hit me hard. I barely knew what to do without her. I had depended on her so much, and now she was just gone! She was such a positive force in our company.

A year later, my assistant Brenda and I were trying hard to find a location to move my offices in Boulder. Jason wouldn't okay it. Finally, we found an office space that Jason had given his okay to, however, it was scratched. Browne didn't want to sign a five-year lease. Later, I discovered that Jason had paid himself a $20,000 bonus. I was angry about that. *How could I not see the handwriting on the wall?*

In the middle of the chaos I was in, my father fell and broke his hip and was in the hospital with pneumonia, lapsing into a coma, and died a few weeks later. I headed to South Dakota to be with him and Mom during this time. I had been scheduled to be in Chicago for the Institute and had to turn everything over to the trainers. A lot of things went wrong. Guess they finally realized how much I really did. It was quite an experience for me and for everyone else.

June 2000

In the summer, I met with Browne and Jason in the Texas offices. There, I got the written bonus package which didn't offer nearly as much as I had expected from our initial agreement. During this meeting, they made it clear that there will be no further live Basic Institutes except those sponsored by a broker dealer going forward. The one concession I got was that the QDRO seminars would be live and in-person. I had to start the tax seminar, adding two new modules: the tax seminar and the creation of a correspondence course with a testing component.

It became clear to me that Browne and Jason didn't believe in personal service. Long before "online meetings" were the norm, they wanted all workbooks to be emailed and downloaded by participants, workbooks that belonged in a 1½ inch binder and cost less than $10 for us to create and mail to each registered attendee.

> The only plus in my life at this time was Bill.

I was really afraid they would run ICDP into the ground. I fantasized about having enough money to buy it back again.

The only plus in my life at this time was Bill. We loved our new home in Longmont and the amazing room we had created with Department 56 ... trains and all. Entertaining was something we both loved and being surrounded by friends warded off the turmoil I faced daily.

Into the third year, the tension and frustration continued to accelerate. Browne put a hold on hiring someone but wouldn't tell me why. Three weeks went by with this question mark looming in my mind. I was scheduled to be in Las Vegas to exhibit at the Financial Services Forum. Bill went with me. We would take an extra day for just us when the show was over. When Isabel got there from Browne's office, she started asking why the shipping and computer work couldn't be handled in Texas. *And then, I realized what Browne had in mind.* And I lost it! How could he?! He was setting me up to *eliminate* me.

> I finally felt Browne's wrath.

The next month, I finally felt Browne's wrath. He screamed at me for 30 minutes over the phone. His choice of profanities was endless. My sin was I had told a student to email me with any concerns. I considered it important to be available and to get feedback. Browne thought otherwise. He considered it to be sabotage. He accused me of going behind his back and building distrust. He treated me like a child.

Depression flowed through my body. It seemed like the Institute was being taken away from me. Browne informed me that Isabel would answer any questions from students and she would decide how the phones would be transferred to their offices. Our database, website, and 800 phone number were under their control. I was to ship all of our computers to their office in Texas. Neither Brenda nor I could access anything.

Jason then called. "Your office is closed and Brenda is fired." She would have no severance. There was no vacation pay for a woman who had been my trusted employee for seven years. They refused to pay the business expenses and since they were on my credit cards, guess who had to pay them?

Then Browne called my loan. I said, "Wait a minute. That's the purchase price for my company. You can't ask that I give it back to you!"

His answer stunned me. "It was a loan. Read the fine print."

Time went on and tensions grew worse. Ugly words and threats came at me nonstop. I got an attorney and we ended up in court in their state.

Meanwhile, I was still their employee, delivering the live seminars for the Institute. I also had individual clients that I worked with separately. More headaches and downing painkillers to offset the never-ending throbbing in my head.

It was a few months before I found myself in front of a judge in his home state. When we got to court, they presented their side first. Then there was a short break of less than 30 minutes before we would present our side of the case.

When we came back from the break, the judge announced, "You don't have to present your side. I have already made my decision." *What? How could he have decided anything? Did something happen during the break?*

I could not believe it! We still believe that Browne's company, worth millions, had swayed the court. The ruling was that I owed the $375,000 plus interest, and Browne had no liability toward me. The attorney for Browne was chuckling when he heard the verdict.

During the two trips to Texas for the court hearings, my mother died. I was a mess.

And on top of that, Bill's company had run up so much debt that we had to file for bankruptcy. Browne and his attorney were no longer chuckling. He wasn't getting his money back.

I was no longer associated with ICDP and I was very concerned about the people I had trained who had become my friends and trusted associates. They all supported me and urged me not to quit the profession. I received more than 55 letters from the CDPs who went through the training.

Their words heartened me during this horrific time.

CDP Robin V. wrote, "I just heard. I am stunned to learn that you are no longer affiliated with ICDP! How can that be? You *are* the ICDP!"

CDP Rita B. added, "I just heard you are no longer with ICDP. I am very saddened by the news. What does that mean to those of us in the program?"

CDP Chris D. added, "Because of the surprise and non-disclosure of your departure from ICDP, I can only think you were blindsided, in some way, within the framework of the organization you strove so diligently to develop. I offer my willingness to support you in whatever manner you need."

"I was very happy with the original setup and with Carol Ann's participation. I was distressed to see the group handed off to new owners who do not appear to be serving either members or the public very well. Certainly, members have heard nothing of value from the new entity and the website doesn't lend any help."

And CDP Ted B. said, "I can't conceive of practicing divorce without you. I don't know what ICDP is doing for us but it's not much. What am I paying them for? We don't get any updates or advice."

So, I studied the tax issues in Canada and started another company there doing exactly the same thing except under a different name. Then Browne sued me for the Canadian company. I transferred the company to two Canadian women and they took it over.

After my year of non-compete ran out, I started another company in the US. It was called Certified Divorce Specialist (CDS). To the previous graduates of ICDP, I updated them on what I was doing and offered to grandfather them into the new certification. Afterall, I and the team I trusted had trained them. I knew they were qualified. And I just felt that I was making a difference. I had found a way to make divorce more equitable and I was determined to do what I felt was right. I come back to that comment by an attorney in Denver, "Carol Ann Wilson's work in the financial issues of divorce has changed family law in Colorado." And it had for so many ... for the financial planning community and for the clients they served.

Letters from previous grads about my new company fortified my decision to reach out and include them.

Now CDP Susan M. wrote, "I'm so happy you are back. It's been lonely and confusing without you. I can't wait to work together again. Thanks so much for moving forward and not leaving me out to dry."

When I got this note from CDP Rebel R., "Glad you have surfaced. I will follow CAW to the end," a broad smile crossed my face.

CDP Susan R. added, "Way to go! Glad you're back, no help from ICDP. I'm really looking forward to working with this new entity."

CDP Lisa W. was thrilled to have me return. "This is great! Glad to see you back in the game. Looking forward to your mentoring once again."

And CDP Judy R. had me laughing out loud. "I'm glad you finally had an attack of good judgment. Why you ever went with that snake, I'll never know."

Browne continued to sue me for nits that went nowhere. It just kept costing me money for attorneys.

I watched their website and eventually found that they were selling a book on divorce that looked suspiciously like the two books that Ed Schilling and I had written together. So, I bought a copy to look it over. Guess what! It was our book with their name on it! Well, here we go again. It was time for another attorney. After many filings back and forth, I flew again to their state to meet with them and the judge, who just happened to be the same judge as the one who had decided my fate. The outcome was that we could continue to sell our books and even reprint them. They could continue to sell the remaining inventory of "their" book but could not reprint it.

I was running my new company and it was competing with theirs (the one they "bought" from me). Of course, they were spreading negative rumors about me. It just didn't let up.

At a national financial conference, a representative from National Underwriters spoke to me and asked if I would be willing to write the book on financial issues in divorce. I was thrilled! She said she would get back to me after the conference. Weeks went by and I hadn't heard anything, so I finally called her. She apologized and said they had chosen to go with two others who would be writing the book. They were in cahoots with Browne. Well, I thought, *It is what it is.*

> With a heavy heart, I stopped being involved with my original company.

When the book was published, I bought a copy. And what a surprise! *It was Almost ALL of my material!* It was time for a copyright attorney and sending lots of copies to National Underwriters. They realized I was correct and pulled the book off the market. Served them right!

Can you believe this? After all this, Browne's group asked me three times if I would come back and run their new company! They can't seem to make it work. They were offering $90,000 per year. I just laughed.

Finally, I made the decision to stop beating my head against a wall. I couldn't compete with Browne's group or anyone who worked for and with him. I turned my certification program over to CDP Deb Johnson, a financial planner in Denver. Deb had gone through my training and became one of my best trainers.

With a heavy heart, I stopped being involved with my original company. I had created a new entity called Real Estate Divorce Specialists and partnered with an attorney, Gregg Greenstein to produce it. It was based on a couple of little known tax laws that benefited couples in divorce who were buying or selling their house in divorce. Realtors did not know about these laws and neither did divorce attorneys! I could hardly believe it! This new company really took off.

Gregg and I are still running this company today.

18
The Tiger Cruise

*This will be the longest time
we will be away from each other.*

When Scott was in the Navy, he would be deployed for six month periods, mostly in the Middle East. His aircraft carrier would return to San Diego via Honolulu. The Navy would allow family members to board the carrier in Honolulu and ride it back to San Diego, usually a six day trip. It was an incredible way for us to see what actually happened on one of these ships.

In the summer of 2005, Scott invited me to go on the Tiger Cruise the upcoming September, in addition to my ex's children, Nicole and Michael, Scott's half sister and brother. I was so excited. We immediately made plans that Bill would fly to San Diego to meet me when our ship reached port. Then we would have a few days to enjoy San Diego and celebrate his 65th birthday.

As I was rushing around to get ready to leave for the airport, Bill came up to me, turned me around and just looked into my eyes. Didn't say anything—just looked into my eyes for the longest time. I just stayed with the moment. He had never done this before. He finally said, "This will be the longest time we will be away from each other." We then hugged and kissed. Oh, what prophetic words!

It was exciting to board the ship—the aircraft carrier USS Boxer. It was as long as three football fields and carried helicopters, LCACs (landing craft), tanks, and much more.

Family members making the trip back to the US are called Tigers. Women tigers had a berthing section to themselves that included the large bathroom facility with showers. The shower was so tight, you could not raise your arms without them going outside of the shower.

> **I was on an adventure of a lifetime.**

The bunks were three high. I had a middle bunk—a whopping 15 inches from mattress to ceiling. I could not even rise up on an elbow once in my bunk. Each of us had another four inches under our mattress that was used for storage—essentials and clothes. To access the space, I needed to raise the heavy mattress. Above my head was a reading light and I could feel air circulating around me that let me know that there was air conditioning. Across the opening was a curtain.

The Ritz it wasn't. Our quarters would not be the poster child for privacy. Yet, I was on an adventure of a lifetime.

It was impossible to get away from the noise of the engines. It was constant. I thought I would go nuts trying to find a quiet place to read. Then I just gave in and read anyway, wherever I was. The Mess always had a movie going. There was always motion; sailors coming and going. Scott's office always had the TV on, even when we were playing poker!

The US Boxer and the Killer Tomato

Today we killed the Killer Tomato. This consisted of a huge bright orange balloon that was about 12 feet across. The crew pushed it off the deck and then the captain proceeded to turn the carrier around. One purpose of this exercise: It took so long to turn this ship around that sailors could see it would be impossible to look for a man overboard. Secondly, it was to give the sailors a chance to identify and destroy an enemy threat.

I was to meet Scott, Nicole and Michael in the Chief's Mess but they weren't there so I started off to where I thought we would be. I ended up on the Bridge and then went out to the Starboard Bridgeway and made myself comfortable—a place I shouldn't have been. I realized that I was standing next to Captain Tom Culara. There were a few other high-ranking people there as well. Five of the Tigers seemed to be personal friends of the captain but I stayed anyway.

The first tomato sank and we couldn't find it. Within minutes, a second inflated one was launched. The next thing I heard was a series of loud shots when the tomato was found. The machine guns had blown it to smithereens.

The experience of the Killer Tomato was unforgettable and so was what happened after the exercise was completed. Another ship came alongside to refuel the Boxer. It shot a line across and then long black hoses snaked across between the ships and were secured by the Boxer. It was really something to watch. Both ships slowed to 13 knots during the two-hour process. I learned that the US is the only country with this technology to refuel ships while the ships are moving. Other countries have to bring the ships to a complete stop.

Anguish at Sea

It was Saturday, September 10, 2005. Scott, Nicole, Michael and I had just finished eating dinner and were sitting at the table talking. One of the men came in and approached Scott. I thought I heard him say that the captain wanted to see him. As Scott left,

I joked with the kids that because I had been naughty and crashed the captain's private party on the Bridge earlier that day, he was probably going to tell him to keep his mother in line and remind me of the ship's protocol.

I hadn't heard correctly. It wasn't the captain who wanted to speak with Scott, rather it was the chaplain. Within five minutes, Scott was back and said, "I need to talk to you privately."

> I need to talk to you privately.

"Should we come, too?" Nicole asked.

"No, just Mom."

As I followed him down the long, narrow hallways and over bulkheads, l said to myself … *it's Bill.*

Following Scott, we entered the chaplain's office. The room was empty. We entered another private room, and Scott turned to close the door behind us and I said, "It's Bill."

He turned with tears in his eyes. "Mom, the chaplain has received word that Bill died."

I cried out loud, "No, no, no, no, no, no!" and fell into his arms. We were both crying. I stepped back, tears flowing, and said loudly, "It's a mistake. He's just hurt, right?"

Scott affirmed that he had died and then I started asking my endless questions.

"What happened? Where did it happen? How did it happen? Why did it happen?" I could not believe anything that was just said … what was being said.

Scott had a slip of paper with Louie's, my son-in-law and Marie's husband, number on it. I had to get to a phone to start making calls. Scott took me to the captain's office and I started calling on a day that I never expected to come. Getting an open line was a continual challenge, dialing dozens of times to find one. For hours, I talked and cried with my family: Louie, Cheryl, Victoria, Mary Margaret, Dick, and I don't even remember who all else. Scott never left my side.

When I finally connected with the coroner, the rest of what happened began to unfold. It appeared that Bill had been struck down with a heart attack either Tuesday or Wednesday morning as he was getting dressed and died in his chair in our bedroom.

> They both knew something was wrong.

Earlier in the week, he had invited Cheryl to go to the CU football game slated for the following Saturday afternoon. Bill had suggested that she come to the house at noon and they would have lunch together. When she arrived and couldn't get in, she turned around to go home then looked back. *Something nudged her to stop. Something is not right.* She went to our neighbor Jill who had a spare key. Her husband Ken accompanied Cheryl to our house.

Opening the door, they both knew something was wrong, horribly wrong. The odor when they opened the front door was overwhelming. Both ascended the stairs and went into the bedroom. As a nurse, Cheryl knew what she was looking at. In front of them was Bill, slumped in the chair, four days after his death. She called the coroner and then set out to find me. All she knew was that I was with Scott on an aircraft carrier in the middle of the Pacific Ocean.

Finally, I realized that I couldn't talk without breaking down. "Can I go someplace private where I could cry by myself?" I asked Scott. He took me to behind where the LCACs (hover crafts) were located. The ship's noise was so loud that I could be as loud as I wished, as loud as I needed to be. I cried hard. I cried out to Bill that I was so sorry. I was sorry that he was alone. I was sorry that I wasn't there for him.

Sleep didn't come to me that night. The next day, a Sunday, I felt like a zombie. I spent hours trying to change my plane ticket to go home on the first plane I could get on and a thousand other details. The remoteness I was in left me feeling helpless. Everything was going on at home without me. *And they were doing it for me.* I felt so useless.

The only way to get me off the ship early was by helicopter, definitely not a small feat in the middle of an ocean. I learned that the carrier would need to be within 100 miles of land to use one of the ship's Delta helicopters to transport me to San Diego. Finally, confirmation came through. Monday would be our exit day. Now I could make firm travel plans.

I am grateful for the care the Navy extended to me and my family—Scott, Nicole, and Michael—as they shepherded the four of us off the ship and into a helicopter, one that was outfitted to carry 30 troops with space for equipment as well. We wore helmets with earmuffs that almost deadened the sound completely. In less than an hour, we landed at the Miramar Air Station. Scott's wife Evelyn picked us up and took me to the San Diego Airport for my flight home to Colorado.

The following day, I went to the house. I knew I would need to pick up some things but what? I dreaded going there. What would I find? My mind was floating in and out.

When I entered the bedroom, it was empty. The bed was gone; the rug had been removed. A bare floor was in front of me with a huge stain that had spread on the flooring. The entire house had to be fumigated; the bedroom carpet would be replaced. And all the clothes in the closets had to be washed or dry cleaned, amounting to 20 bags!

While I was there, the fumigation team arrived to start the cleanup and sanitizing, informing me that I could probably get back in within a couple of days. That was something I was anxious to do—to get back into my home. After inspecting the floor, they recommended replacing it completely. That would take another week. So be it. I would live with rugs on plywood floors until them. Another company came to clean out the air ducts.

When would I feel whole again?

It's amazing what the shock of losing someone does to your body. I couldn't think or remember things. I just couldn't concentrate. No matter how normal I acted, on the inside I was a wreck. My emotions were right on the surface. And certain words or situations became triggers and could cause the tears to flow immediately. I was exhausted most of the time.

How does one explain the physical impact to one's body? I couldn't. All I knew was that I wasn't myself and some of my spark

With children Marie, Scott, and Cheryl after Bill's funeral

had been diminished ... a spark that ignited my physical energy to go forward when long hours were needed and one that normally fueled my *can do* attitude.

I think that the loss must feel greater when the love was much greater. I always felt that Bill was my other half, and truly he was. So, it felt as though half of me had been ripped away. I felt like half a person.

When would I feel whole again?

19
Machu Picchu

<small>Oh sure, you don't really know how I feel.</small>

Bill died in September 2005. I tried to return to work but my usual efficiency escaped me. Forgetfulness became my new norm. My assistant, Brenda Bates, told me that I needed to take time to heal. *Take time*, I thought ... *I needed to be back at work.*

A few months later, my car engine started shouting at me. A variety of weird noises poured through its hood. Cars weren't my area of responsibility. It's for the car guys. One of Bill's friends from the Barbershoppers was JR. He said, "Take it to Sonny's Garage. He's the best there is. Sonny is honest and fair." That was exactly what I needed to hear. It was January in Colorado and no one wants car trouble in the winter. I made an appointment with Sonny's Garage before January was over.

When I went to pick up my car, Sonny was the one I interacted with when I paid the bill. For some reason, I shared with him that my husband had recently died and that he always took care of the car. And now, I had that task.

Sonny stopped working on the paperwork connected to my repairs, looked up and said, "I know how you feel."

WHAT! I immediately thought, *Oh sure, you don't really know how I feel.*

Then Sonny finished his sentence, "My wife was killed by an impaired driver two weeks ago while she was out walking."

Oh, my gosh! I was almost speechless.

Then, he came out from behind the counter and walked me to my car. *He did understand.* We stood and talked with tears streaming down both our cheeks. During those 15 minutes of sharing, Sonny mentioned that maybe we could have coffee sometime to talk more.

So, we did. In fact, we met several times to talk after that first reveal of our common bond. One evening, I invited him for dinner and we each told our stories. This time it was the storyline of the marriages we both had had. He came from a loving marriage as I had and our talk was filled with emotion. More tears flowed as we cried together and shouted at the universe and the unfairness of it all. This went on for months.

Exactly one year after Bill's death, I was crying thinking about his being dead in our bedroom for four days before anyone found him. It was more than I could bear. I called Sonny and he came right over and held me while I cried. Sonny really helped me through this, as I helped him. I guess we were each other's therapists while grieving and healing.

Machu Picchu

Several months after Bill died, I heard about a group from Boulder going to Machu Picchu. Oh, I had always wanted to go but Bill was never interested. Was this my chance? Was it too soon?

I met with Kevin Haight, an attorney in Boulder who was leading the group, his 25th excursion! One of my concerns was the extensive hike in over the Inca Trail, which was well-known to be a daunting physical trip. Could I do it? Would my ileostomy be a problem? We talked about the conditions and the challenges and my physical abilities. He convinced me that it would not be a problem.

With his encouragement, I signed up on the spot!

> My eyes absorbed them as if I were a child at play.

During a coffee visit, I shared with Sonny my desire to someday see Machu Picchu, and that I had signed up for a group tour in the summer. "I've been there" was his response.

That got my attention. "Let's share pictures when I get back."

June 18, 2006, was the beginning of my long awaited adventure as I boarded the flight to Lima, Peru, then on to Cusco, where we stayed for a week to acclimate ourselves to the altitude of 11,152 feet.

We spent most of our time while in Cusco bussing to archeological wonders nearby. There seemed to be no limit to them. My eyes absorbed them as if I were a child at play.

Then it was time to pack for our trip. The trek from Cusco to Machu Picchu would take four days walking, passing over two mountain passes at 13,779 and finally ending at Machu Picchu with an elevation of 7,792 feet for a total of 26 miles.

Peruvian porter

There were Peruvian porters who would take our bags and all the equipment for the trek. This included tents, latrines, cooking equipment, food, sleeping bags, air mattresses and anything else that we would need. Our personal bag could weigh no more than 55 pounds. Before we departed, each in the group was required to weigh his or her bag. Anything over 55 pounds had to be left behind. We had our own day backpacks for whatever was personally considered essential. I was grateful for the detailed list of recommended items to include.

The first day was relatively easy. We hiked about seven miles during which we gained roughly 1,200 feet before camp.

The second day added eight miles, not much more than the first, but more demanding. I could feel the gain in the climb, another 3,500 feet, all moderate to somewhat steep. We crossed over Dead Women Pass then descended fairly steeply 1,800 feet to the overnight camp at 11,800 feet.

The third day was another up and down day, another seven miles starting with a 1,000 foot climb to the top of the second pass. A gradual, easy ascent followed to the final camp before our destination of the mysterious Machu Picchu that had called to me for years. The new altitude was 12,200 feet.

> **My knees felt each step.**

With the 360-degree view, the sunrises and sunsets were absolutely stunning, indescribable really. Taking a deep breath, I could feel that I was healing. As my eyes took in the views, what was in front of me was as great as it could get.

The fourth and last day completed the final leg, adding an additional four miles while on the Inca Trail. The good news for me was that it was almost all downhill or level, and actually took only about a half day of time. The first three miles were uncomfortable as the descent was moderate to steep, and unrelenting for about 2,000 feet. My knees felt each step.

As I think back, the camps had been wonderful. When we arrived at our destination each afternoon, my tent was set up and waiting for me, with foam mattress, sleeping bag, and my duffle bag already inside. The porters would have already placed hot water by my tent for washing up. Next, I would head to the dining tent for snacks and tea with the rest of the group, which numbered six. Dinners had been surprisingly delicious and beautiful. The salads would be arranged like flowers, a lovely touch.

Each morning, I was awakened by "the scratch of the puma" on my tent door—the puma being a porter—who brought me a mug of hot tea. He was followed shortly after by another porter bringing more hot water for more washing, and then came breakfast in the dining tent. This may include French toast, bananas flambe, or cereal. While the group breakfasted, the porters took down the campsite, packing everything up. Normally, our group would start out on the day's hike before the porters did. Within a few hours, they would pass us, racing to get to the next stopping place to set up camp again before we all arrived.

And then our visual treat rolled out. The porters were like mountain goats as they leaped and bounded from one rock to the next, always maintaining perfect balance, with their backs loaded with equipment, food, and our individual bags. There were ten of them ... and six of us.

There was a rule that a foreign tour leader like Kevin must hire a local licensed guide to accompany any group. So, Kevin hired Dimas and then if a policista surfaced and demanded to see Kevin's guide license, he could simply point to Dimas and say, "He's the guide. I'm just the tour leader." End of problem.

There was another advantage for our group. We got two different viewpoints on a subject matter involving Machu Picchu. Dimas was more familiar with folklore about the Incas than Kevin was, while Kevin's background in modern archeology and scientific investigation of the mysteries was stronger and more recent than

Dimas' was. So, with both of them, my group got the benefit of two perspectives.

Finally, the big day arrived. We hiked into Machu Picchu, one of the seven wonders of the modern world. And what an amazing and breathtaking site to see … to be there … and to think about the civilization that lived there more than five and a half centuries ago!

> I felt the energy around me.

Machu Picchu

Our group had been given the OK to hike around the area independently so I took advantage of it. I moved up and down stairs, weaving in and out of the many rooms, and all the time experiencing the environment and scenery that enveloped the area. I loved watching the llamas munching on grass in the center area.

Finally, I wanted to find a private spot to sit and meditate. I just wanted to think, to feel, to be alone. It was a challenge with the hundreds of people roaming around the area. But I did find my spot. For 30 minutes, I settled in. Then, I pulled out a little 2x2 inch plastic bag I had carried with me, close to me, from Colorado. In it were some of Bill's ashes. "Bill, I know you didn't want to make this hike, so I brought you with me." I then emptied the ashes onto the ground.

I felt the energy around me and that of many others. I felt Bill with me: his smile, his humor, his caring.

It was time to leave this amazing place. As my group headed to the buses that would bring us to a nearby hotel, the word *exhilaration* was the common bond we all shared. Each of us had a different take, yet all of us added Machu Picchu to our "experiences of a lifetime" list. We stayed overnight then bussed back to Cusco the next morning where another exciting adventure awaited.

There was one more archeological dig to explore. This one was an active site and Gordon McEwen was the director, a nationally known archeologist and a leading expert on the Incas. While there, one of McEwen's graduate students unearthed a skull. Gordon didn't seem too excited. He said they always find lots of skulls. But for me, and for my group, it would be a special remembrance.

My trek to Machu Picchu on the original trail and the rock pavers that tilted in complete disorder was one of the most exciting experiences I've ever had. At the same time, it was extraordinarily difficult for me ... probably the most difficult physical activity I'd ever done.

I was so pleased and proud of myself for doing it!

20
Recovering

*We argued back and forth a bit and then I said,
"How much do you want to bet?"*

After Bill died, I wanted to do something to memorialize him. I have always been an advocate of education, of books, of reading to children. As a member of Rotary and supportive of its scholarship program, I thought, *Why can't I host dinners to raise money for scholarships? Cooking is easy for me and it would be fun as well.*

And so, I did. I started promoting "Have dinner at Carol Ann's and help raise money for the Bill Fullmer Scholarship Fund." I ran the money through the Rotary scholarship committee as they had the means to select the recipients.

Aa many as 20 people would sign up for any of the several dinners I cooked. We raised enough to award ten scholarships! Even Tyler Brayton, our football player Bill and I sponsored, sent a check for $2,000.

One dinner included Captain Alfred McLaren. We knew him as Fred, retired from the USN, a veteran of more than 20 Cold War missions and three Arctic expeditions. He was awarded the Distinguished Service Medal and two Legions of Merit as a Cold War submarine commander, a Rotarian and our friend. He entertained us after dinner with his slides of his two dives to the Titanic.

Four of us women in Rotary had lost our husbands that year. I had mused out loud, "Is it a risk for a married woman to join

Rotary?" We shared some of the thoughts that we had and what others had said to us:

"You're used to living alone so you'll be OK."

"How long are you going to wear your wedding rings?"

"What are some good things that have come from this?"

This last one almost made me want to slap her! But my pain and loss of Bill was too deep. As a psychotherapist, her question was mind-numbing to me. From Joan Didion's book, *The Year of Magical Thinking*, she writes:

> We might expect if the death is sudden to feel shock. We might expect that we will be prostrate, inconsolable, crazy with loss. We do not expect to be literally crazy, cool customers who believe that their husband is about to return and need his shoes.

And from my journal:

> But now it's past. And it's time for me to move on. It's time for me to get busy and create a new life, a new business. I've been reading books, listening to tapes and making lists. I can do this! Time to develop a positive mental attitude. Time to create my future. I will!

Bolder Boulder 10K Race

I looked forward to every Memorial Day, as did thousands of Boulderites and mega thousands from around Colorado and all over the world. It was time for the annual Bolder Boulder 10K race. I ended up race-walking in 25 of them. I race-walked my last one at 80 years old! I loved that time of year because it became family time.

> Would you like to get a cup of coffee or something, sometime this week?

Both Scott and Marie would fly home to run the race with their race-walking mom. When Bill was alive, his form of movement was jogging, so we composed a band of runners, joggers, and racewalkers. It was perfect.

The Bolder Boulder was a big deal ... and still is. It became party time in Boulder. The runners would wear costumes and there was a band on every block for entertainment.

There could be more than 40,000 people from all over the world who would come to enter this race.

The organizers started "the wave" as a way to ensure that the runners wouldn't feel so crowded. The numbers on our bibs told us what wave we were in. The waves started every one minute with 200 people in each wave. Many just wanted to participate to have a good time. We started first in order to clear the way for the serious runners, the pros that were competing for money.

top: Racewalking the Bolder Boulder

left: With Marie in our Bolder Boulder costumes

Wheelchair participants were welcomed as well as military bases from all over the world. We had "shoe cards" placed under our shoelaces that monitored our times as we crossed computerized strips throughout the 10K run or 6.2 miles.

The wave method was copycatted by other organizers of large races. I learned long ago that smart people don't have to reinvent things that work.

I wrote in my journal in October 2006:

> I called Sonny last week and said, "Would you like to get a cup of coffee or something, sometime this week?" He said sure and suggested dinner the following evening. We spent two and one-half hours talking about everything. He is really a nice guy and I expect I'll be seeing him again as he was so pleasant to be with. To have a friend to do things with would be wonderful.

And I did see him again, and again, and again. Several months later, we decided that we really liked each other and started dating. We are still together after 16 years! We have never married, each living in our own house, but we are a solid couple. When asked by our friends why we don't get married, my answer is always the same. "Why? This works so well. After not seeing each other for a couple of days, we are excited to see each other again."

Sonny Stratton comes from a family of five boys raised by a single mom. He is the middle son and a natural leader, creating Sonny's Garage almost 50 years ago. A car guy and collector of vintage cars, I always know where to find him: his warehouse that is filled with cars. Obviously, we go to lots of car shows where he enters one of his "show cars." There are lots of local ones, and then the ones that are "must be there" on the West and East coasts.

> **I think you're allergic to me!**

A native Coloradan with most of his life in Longmont, he knows most everybody and everybody knows him. Comments like, "We just *love* Sonny!" easily spill from the lips of others. Known for his generosity and caring, Sonny is definitely one who a friend can call at 3 a.m.! I am blessed to have him in my life.

An interesting thing happened when I first started spending time with him. On several occasions, I would start coughing and sneezing until he finally said, "I think you're allergic to me!" This made me laugh.

Mike is my chiropractor and known for unusual techniques for healing my many problems. When I mentioned this to him, he said, "Bring in one of Sonny's work shirts." This also made me laugh. But I brought a work shirt on my next visit. Mike placed it over my face while doing chiropractic maneuvers. Suddenly, my head cleared up immediately. Mike said, "I believe you had a traumatic experience around the smell of oil at some time."

"Do you think it had anything to do with learning about my husband's death while on an aircraft carrier?"

He said, "Bingo!"

The allergies never returned.

New Ventures

It was time for me to get going again. I didn't have my companies that I started any longer to create the revenues I had. And I still needed to make a living. There's a well-known saying, Go with what brung you. And what brung me was information. I had so much to share with others.

I had never thought of myself as being in the "information" business, but that is what I was and am. My assistant and I developed a seminar for CPAs and another tax class for financial planners. We mailed out brochures on each seminar and started getting signups. I also developed The Thursday Teleclass series for financial planners in my area of expertise: divorce. They paid to listen as I interviewed experts on many different subjects:

maintenance, dividing retirement plans, working with attorneys, QDROs, courtroom procedures, splitting the house, and many more. This was quite popular and was another stream of income along with all the seminars I was doing.

I met with attorney Gregg Greenstein about starting a certification course for realtors called Real Estate Divorce Specialists. It really took off and we are still running it today. I started exhibiting at Real Estate conventions and we almost became a household name.

I started teaching goals classes: *Reach Your Dreams* and *Setting, Achieving and Surpassing Your Goals*.

I taught seminars for women: *Financial Empowerment for Women* and *Women, Power and Money*.

I developed talks for the public: *What to Do When Goal Setting Does Not Work* and *Financial Transitions in Your Life*. This last talk was interesting. It had four subheads: Changing Jobs, Getting Married, Death of a Spouse, and Divorce. The audience would listen politely to the first three subheads, possibly taking notes. But when I hit Divorce, the hands were flying up with questions!

I sent out flyers to financial planning firms across the nation offering to speak at their meetings. They paid my expenses and in return, I sold my books and signed up people for my classes. I also spoke to attorney groups that resulted in more client cases. I was becoming quite busy and starting to travel again.

It was a good thing for me personally ... and for those who I could share my "information" with.

Pioneer Award

In 2008, I received an unexpected and delightful phone call, quickly followed up with written notification. The Association of Financial Divorce Planners, a membership association, was honoring me with the prestigious Pioneer Award for outstanding contributions to the field of divorce. And what an honor it was. I was flown to New York with all expenses paid to accept the award and to give a speech. It was such a wonderful tribute to me and the path I had created. I was in a state of euphoria as I connected with and hugged old and new friends, most of whom had gone through my training.

While in New York, I stayed with Barbara Stark at her apartment in Brooklyn. From her tiny deck, you could look over the Hudson River and see the Statue of Liberty. It was the first time I learned what it was really like to live in such a dense population. It could take as long as 30 minutes to find a parking place within six blocks. There was a small grocery store next to a dry cleaners, a coffee shop, and a bakery, all within a short walking distance. Definitely convenient.

Scott's Retirement

Also in 2008, my son Scott retired from the Navy after 22 years. Sonny and I flew to San Diego for the ceremony. What an elaborate presentation! He was praised for his enormous contribution to the Navy. The empty table for fallen men was there. Scott was presented with his "Shadow Box." His shadow box was in the shape of a ship's steering wheel and under the glass was displayed his ribbons, medals, his commendations, the flag, and other memorabilia. He followed with his

Scott at his retirement showing his "shadow box."

farewell speech that included a challenge for his teammates he was leaving behind. Finally, he "exited" through a double line of his men. It was an emotional event. With tears flowing throughout, I was so proud of what he had accomplished.

After the ceremony, the whole family—eight of us—went to dinner at a nice restaurant. When it was time to pay, we told the servers that we were paying for Scott and his wife, Evelyn, so they should split their bill between the rest of us. Well, they just couldn't figure this out. They said the computer couldn't do that. It became a bit complicated, but we finally got the bill paid. The next night we went to a different restaurant. We had a wonderful time talking and laughing. After a long time went by, we couldn't figure out why we hadn't been presented with the bill. Finally, it came out. Sonny had taken care of it. He didn't want a redo of the previous evening!

> **I became a poker player!**

Later in the year, I was booked to give a talk in San Francisco. Sonny came along and we stayed several extra days to tour the city and surrounding area, including Napa Valley to taste the wines. It was a magical time. When it was time to leave, we were sitting in the waiting area at the airport and I actually fell asleep while sitting up straight. Something woke me and I said, "I fell asleep."

Sonny answered, "I know you did."

"How did you know?"

"You weren't talking."

I cracked up!

And would you believe, I became a poker player! *And I mean a serious poker player.* I started playing free poker at the Bit of Billiards, known by the locals as The Bit, playing twice a week to learn and to become better. And I did.

Playing poker in Las Vegas.

Now, I play in tournaments three times a week here in Longmont at the American Legion. I go to Blackhawk up in the Rocky Mountains on a regular basis. And I go to Las Vegas frequently.

Sonny has been the captain of a bowling team for more than 46 years. Each year, the national bowling tournament is held in Las Vegas, Reno, or Baton Rouge. So, each year we go for four days to a city that has casinos! He bowls and I gamble. What a treat.

December 2009

Sonny and I went to the CU-Nebraska football game at the CU stadium. Going down the steep steps to our seats in Row 2, I pitched forward on the concrete steps. I fractured my knee bone, sprained my wrist, and bruised some ribs. The miracle was that I got my left hand up in front of my face just in time because my face was headed for the metal bleacher seat. If I hadn't, I would have either split open my chin or knocked my teeth out. Still, I hit the bleacher hard. By the fourth quarter, I was in so much pain that we left. A brace became my inseparable companion for almost three months.

Sonny and I belonged to a dinner club and I showed up, still stiff and braced up at the February dinner. Revealing to my companions, I said, "I'm anxious to get out of my brace so I can start training for the Bolder Boulder in May."

Amused, one friend said, "Oh no, you're not going to do the Bolder Boulder!"

"Oh, yes I am!"

We argued back and forth a bit and then I said, "How much do you want to bet?"

"$5.00!"

Right then and there, we wrote up our agreement and both signed it. We took it around the room and eight more people signed it, all agreeing to pony up $5.00 each if I made it.

May arrived and I did the Bolder Boulder, and it was easy! The physical training I started in February did the trick. At the next dinner club in June, I went around and collected my five dollars from everyone who had signed the paper.

One of Those Days

Did you ever have one of those days? Well, actually, this all happened in the same week. First, my water heater went out and I had to replace it to the tune of $2,000. Then my kitchen cupboard fell off the wall and my dishes crashed down, some of which were irreplaceable. Then my computer mouse stopped working. Next, my computer crashed, a major problem. Then my phone stopped working. Then I had to buy a new printer. Then I had to buy a new router. Oh well, it is what it is.

Happenings with Friends and Family

Longmont has many events for the public. We try to go to most of them. The main street is closed down for four blocks with vendors, bands, trampolines for the kids, and food. So, Sonny's son Jeff and his fiancée Sheila brought his two kids and her two kids. Then Sonny's first wife and her new husband, and Sonny and I went to the street festival. The ten of us were like an amoeba moving through the crowd, always staying together. Then we had dinner at a restaurant and laughed about how Jeff triple-dated with his parents and their boyfriend/girlfriend!

There are also two family events that happen every year. In August is the family picnic on the acreage at Gary (Sonny's brother) and Sharron's house. Everyone brings food, and tent shelters are set up to eat under. We have always been blessed with nice, sunny weather.

The second event is in December at Sonny's house. Everyone brings food and a gift to exchange. The family is growing and there are almost always thirty people in attendance. We play bingo until everyone has had a bingo and can choose a gift from under the tree. We also allow "stealing" from each other. You can imagine the shouts and screams of joy and laughter. The children love this event and it is amazing to see how much they have grown from the previous year.

Life goes on, again. Cheryl's husband Cliff died in 2011 of complications of diabetes. And in 2014, Cheryl married Ken Brecko. And Scott's wife Evelyn died in a car crash in 2017. Then Scott married Petra in 2020.

Ladies Celebration Lunch

Along with aging comes the loss of friends. After hearing of the death of another one of my favorite people, I realized I had not reached out to my friends in a long time. More importantly, I had never told them how much their friendship meant to me. I had not shared many memories that they might enjoy hearing about.

I planned a gathering in July 2013 of the women who had impacted my life, starting with my sister, Mary Margaret, followed by my two daughters, Cheryl and Marie. My thoughts then went to my friends.

The most recent friend was Barb Dunn, who became my "poker buddy" and taught me so much that improved my game as well as becoming a confidant.

There was Kamilla Macar who was my hiking and camping buddy. We spent so many hours in the wilderness together and talked for a zillion hours.

Then my spiritual guru, Marian Head who was always there for me and for anyone else who needed her wise and thoughtful advice. Everyone loved her.

Barbara Stark was absolutely critical in my forming a training company way back at the beginning. I learned about law from her. She believed in me and what I was doing and supported me without hesitation. She was essential to the training seminars with her knowledge and crisp and simple way of explaining complicated situations.

Then there is Judith Briles. Through the years of my struggles, she was there for me. What a dynamo! Including

With friends Judith Briles and Ski Milburn

writing her own 42 books, she has helped dozens of others to write and get published. Judith suggested I write another book on divorce, this time an all-encompassing one. So, I did. What an undertaking! She was my editor, influenced the layout, oversaw the cover design, and then the printing. With her efforts and *pushing* me, the book was available in time for my talk at a large conference.

After I had coordinated everyone's schedules, my sister from North Carolina, Marie from Tucson, Barbara from New York, and Cheryl from Denver, I was ready to wrap gifts and plan the food menu. Everyone received an engraved silver jewelry box. A bowl was passed around for each "honorary guest" to draw a gift and then share what the unique saying meant to her. Then more, then more … I just couldn't quit. And I happily cooked all the food for the luncheon. The day was delicious: foodwise, peppery conversation, and wonderful friends.

After we finished eating, I gave a "little speech" telling about each special person there: who she was; what she meant to me; and interesting things about her.

I had the most fun of all!

The Flood

The flood of September 2013 made national headlines! Sonny's Garage was wiped out. Weeks of rain had caused the river to rise and rush down the canyon. The force of water is tremendous. His shop ended up with three feet of water and we couldn't get in until three feet of mud and debris was shoveled away from the doors.

Just before the main flood of water, Sonny had been cautious. He removed a $22,000 motor that he was going to put into a customer's car and took it to his house. Much of his equipment in his shop was lost. The cleanup of the thousands of tools took a long time. Many of his friends kept coming to help. Finally, he got to the point that he had to turn some away. They all said, "Sonny helped me. Now it's my turn to help him."

This was the rain that washed away most of Jamestown in Colorado. No one could get in or out of the city of Lyons. Stories abounded throughout Colorado about damages and recovery during the massive rains of the month.

Sonny had been thinking about retiring for some time and so he figured the time was now. He owns the buildings and the land outright. After his great cleanup, he would use the building to work on his own cars. Closing the business made sense for him … and he figured this would give him more time to travel.

And travel we did!

21
Hello World ...
Here We Come

Before we left America, I had had visions of long lines of old women dressed in black with black shawls covering their heads.

Well, we finally did it. In 2012, after much discussion, Sonny and I booked an eight day trip on a Viking River Boat Cruise down the Rhine. We went from Basel to Amsterdam and enjoyed the many castles on the shore and the tours of Basel, Breisach, Strasbourg, Heidelberg, Braubach, Koblenz, Cologne, and Kinderdijk. Goodness! We were immersed in culture that surrounded us as we flowed down the river. Throughout the cruise, we were treated to superb four star meals.

After stepping off the final leg of the cruise, we stayed a few more days in Amsterdam. Joan and Paul Schwenke's home was our destination. They took us to Keukenhof Gardens. What an incredible display of acres of flowers.

Two years later, we booked another Viking trip down the river Elbe from Prague to Berlin. When we got to Prague, the weather had been so dry and the river so low, they couldn't get the riverboat to Prague! We had to take a bus to a city downstream to get on ours. In Berlin we saw a portion of the Berlin Wall and the most incredible memorial to the Holocaust. It actually gave me the chills.

We took a couple of extra days to go to Krakow to see Auschwitz. Krakow is a beautiful city and Auschwitz was a sobering experience. While there, we met up with three other couples who had also taken this extended tour. We had no trouble bonding with these interesting and fun people. When we got back to the boat, we sat together at dinner, and thus began a week of laughter.

Introducing ourselves around the table, the woman from Germany revealed how they weren't married, nor did they live together ... but she had the ring! When we asked when they would be married, she replied, "We will never get married and it doesn't matter, because I have *the ring*!" And she extended her hand into the air so we could admire her beautiful diamond while we were choking with laughter. Well, this became the mantra that would lead us into more laughter. We decided to call ourselves "The Krakow Eight."

In 2015, we again booked a Viking trip down the Danube from Nuremberg to Budapest. We *loved* Budapest. It is so beautiful and we loved the baths. I found out that the baths have been found to be so beneficial that doctors will prescribe thirty days for their patients to sit in them. And the unbelievable part is that insurance will pay for their trip including transportation and hotel! We sat in them as long as we could.

The tour director on this trip was a delight. He was so friendly and funny AND he could sing! He even gave a concert for us one evening. He sang a lot of popular songs and then sang opera. What a voice. We thoroughly enjoyed it. I just fell in love with him.

During one of our free times in Budapest, we heard about the Shoe Memorial and spent some time trying to find it. When we did, it was a sobering experience.

Titled *Shoes on the Danube Bank*, it memorializes 3,500 people, 800 of them Jews, who were shot into the Danube during the time of the Arrow Cross terror. Shoes were valuable and could be stolen and resold by the militia after the massacre. They were ordered to take off their shoes and were shot at the edge of the water so that their bodies fell into the river and were carried away. The memorial represents their shoes left behind on the bank.

Each of our experiences on the Viking riverboats added to our memories. In 2016, we headed to Paris to begin our next venture. Our highlights there were the Palace of Versailles and the trip to Giverny and the studio of Claude Monet.

Shoes on the Danube

The surrounding gardens of Monet's workshop were equal to botanic gardens anywhere. It was thrilling to see the actual lily pads on the water and the bridge in the background that I have seen in so many of his paintings.

We chose to add three more days to explore Paris. I had always said that I wanted to sit at an outdoor café on the Champs-Elysees and have a glass of wine and watch the people go by. And so, it came to be. We were tourists bar none and saw as many attractions as we could during our time there. When we walked out of our hotel, we looked directly at the Eiffel Tower. The hotel was interesting. It was a first-class hotel, yet our room had no dresser, no closet and no shelves anyplace. Where were we to put our stuff?

In 2018, our Viking trip took us to Russia, boarding in St. Petersburg and ending in Moscow. Highlights were the Hermitage Museum, the Faberge Museum, the "onion" topped buildings, and the GUM department store—amazing! I've always heard that GUM (pronounced goom) was quite a store, but I had no idea. It covered a huge city block with three stories. When you walk into one of its many entrances, you don't really see a "store." You see a city. There are open aisles about three stories high lined with shops selling "posh" items that nobody can afford. As we went deeper into the building, we found lovely food displays, ice cream vendors in the centers of the aisles, escalators, fancy décor. Our eyes were overwhelmed with what we saw. We tried to take pictures that would show what we were seeing but it was almost impossible.

> We don't talk about him.

Before we left America, I had had visions of long lines of old women dressed in black with black shawls covering their heads. Nothing like that! Those cities are absolutely modern. You would think you were in a large US city: lots of bright colors; kids on their skateboards; music playing. Everything appeared perfectly normal. The only thing I had a problem with was that the guides would not answer my questions that had anything to do with the famous ballet artist, *Rudolf Nureyev.* "*We don't talk about him.*"

The following year was our sixth and last Viking trip to Eastern Europe which included Romania, Bulgaria, Serbia, Croatia, and Hungary. Those small countries were filled with so many beautiful crafts that I wanted to take home almost everything I saw! On one of our tours in Croatia, the tour guide told us about the 95-year-old woman who proudly proclaimed that she has lived in six countries during her life and never left her home! For some reason, Croatia was the country that every conquering power wanted to have. We ended at Budapest where we added three more days so we could see what we missed the first time and to enjoy the baths once again.

Back Home Again …

In July 2014, we took off in Sonny's show car—cherry red 55 Chev—for a car show in Vancouver, Washington. We stopped at lots of casinos along the way. On the way back, because it was the 4th of July weekend, we had a hard time finding a place to stay. We ended up staying in Idaho Falls. We were told that the town's fireworks were the best in the western US. And it was the most amazing display that I had ever seen. They shot out 5-10 fireworks at a time, forming patterns and backgrounds. Designs I'd never seen before filled the whole sky. Hundreds of people come for miles around for this show.

The next year, Sonny's motor home became a home away from home as we headed to Tucson to look things over for a future trip. Liking what we saw, we reserved space for 2016 for a month in Tucson and two months in Mesa. In Tucson, we stayed at the Voyageur RV Resort and what a place. Activities of every kind: bridge, pinochle, mahjong, glass blowing, woodworking, cribbage, and of course, poker three nights a week! In Mesa, we stayed at the Val Vista RV Resort and the activities were all the same, including poker. We loved it! In fact, we are now snow bunnies and we go every winter to Arizona for three months in the motor home, with the exception of this year as I pen this—2022. The Florida Keys became our destination. It took us two months there and back. We followed the coastline along the Gulf to Florida. There was so much to see that it took us a while to get to Key West. We had many experiences along the way.

Quite a bit of time was spent searching for Luckenbach, Texas. Why, you ask. It's the name that Willie Nelson made famous. I had to see what it was all about and just what a sweet little place it was. Our wheels turned toward the River Walk in San Antonio, down to Galveston and on to New Orleans and Biloxi where there are many, many casinos. A few hands of poker beckoned to me. Of course, we spent a few days there.

When we stop, Sonny has to unhook the car from the motor home, and then hook up the electricity, water, and sewer. When we leave a spot, he has to do everything backward. Sonny estimates he has hooked up and unhooked the car about two dozen times, which means he has hooked up and unhooked the utilities about two dozen times. This is all within the first 20 days. I wonder if he thought about this beforehand?

Oh, yes, while we were at the River Walk, I stumbled down a few unlit steps and hurt my arm! After several visits to medical facilities, we found that I actually had broken it. I was in a brace that I had to wear all the time, even to bed. Now Sonny found out about washing dishes, tying my shoes, fastening my bra. Well, you get the picture.

In St. Petersburg, Florida, we went to the Salvador Dali Museum. When we were on the third floor, we noticed a man-sized

Sonny and I at Cheryl's wedding

black panel that looked like the black screen of a computer. We pushed a button and Dali appeared in front of us, talking to us about his art. Later, we saw another screen. We pushed a button and Dali appeared in front of us again talking about the exhibit. Then, as we were leaving the museum, another black screen was visible, so obviously, we pushed the button.

Dali appeared once again and said, "So now you are leaving. I hope you enjoyed the exhibit. But before you go, I would like to take a picture of you." He picked up a camera, aimed it at us, and took a picture. Then, he looked at the picture and said, "Oh, that's very nice." Turning his face toward us, he added, "Would you like to see it?" He then turned the camera around and there we were on his camera! We laughed so hard!

22
My Final Thoughts

Truly, I am blessed.

Looking back is always interesting, isn't it? At 85 years of age, I can see now where the milestones were, and what the results were of certain decisions. And this is what I found.

Having ostomy surgery led to an incredibly fulfilling life. How is that? ... you might wonder. Well, just think about this. After multiple surgeries, I found that I wanted to help others who had had the same surgery. So, I spoke to doctors' groups; I talked to nurses' groups; and I spoke at chapter meetings globally. This developed my speaking skills and took away all fear of speaking. And the bonus was traveling internationally and meeting amazing men and women.

Then came the awareness of the unfairness directed toward women in divorce settlements. I wanted to help them get better results. This resulted in creating a new profession including software that would show the result of any given settlement proposal. It resulted in speaking nationally and in Canada over a span of 30 years. It was gratifying when an attorney said to me, "Carol Ann, I've been telling others in the community and my profession that Carol Ann Wilson's work in the financial issues of divorce has changed family law in Colorado."

The reality is my efforts and software impacted and changed family law nationwide.

Yes, there were some bumps in the road, many of them. Yet, that's life, isn't it? But I overcame them. And the past 16 years with Sonny have been so happy. Who knew that another wonderful man would come into my life after Bill? And I no longer have headaches or coughing spells.

So, what's my takeaway from all of this? What have I learned that I can pass on to you?

Throughout all the pain from the multiple surgeries, I never gave up. I always looked forward to getting better, getting well so I could get back to my family and my children. If you have read Victor Frankl's *Man's Search for Meaning,* you will know that he survived the concentration camps by visualizing his future with his wife and of lecturing after the war regarding lessons to be learned from Auschwitz. That kept him going throughout the beatings, the starvation and the terrible conditions. He survived because of his visualizations. He said, "You cannot control what happens to you, but you can always control what you do about what happens to you."

The second challenge for me was losing my company in a terribly nasty way. I just knew that I had talents that would help others and I was determined to keep using them any way I could. I refused to give up in that darkest of times.

My son Scott said something to me that I must share with you. I was telling him one evening all about my troubles and really filling him in. After I had gone through most of it, he made some comment about how life had really been good to me. I thought, wait a minute. That doesn't compute?! I asked him a couple of times to explain what he meant but he said he couldn't explain what he had been feeling. The next day he came to me and explained.

Mom, you have affected so many other people's lives. You have been involved with them through your volunteer organizations and through business. You have helped other people and have been good to them, therefore life will be good to you and you will always be taken care of.

That from my son!

It's amazing what a change of attitude can do for what used to be ulcer-causing incidents. For instance, if I miss a plane, I think, *well, maybe I was meant to be in this city for two more hours. Maybe the next person I talk to will be instrumental in adding to my life.* Or if I get a flat tire out on the highway, I think, m*aybe the next person who comes along to help change this tire will be someone I am destined to meet.*

Imagine how the acceptance of all events—no matter how irritating—on the basis of expectancy and accepting life can add to the calm and happiness of a person.

In looking back, and going forward, everything in my life has led to incredible adventures with people, organizations and experiences.

Truly, I am blessed.

About Carol Ann Wilson

Carol Ann is best known for her work in constructing more equitable financial divorce settlements. In addition to creating a new profession, she has written nearly a dozen books on the financial issues in divorce. She has spoken on this subject hundreds of times to rapt audiences.

A second area of expertise is her involvement with the ostomy associations internationally. She has formed many ostomy chapters, served on the National Board of the United Ostomy Association, and was a founder of the International Ostomy Association.

Carol Ann is the author of several books including *The Financial Advisor's Guide to Divorce Settlement*, *The Survival Manual for Women in Divorce*, *The Ultimate Guide to Surviving Your Divorce*, and coauthor of *The Dollars and Sense of Divorce*.

She is proud of having climbed two fourteeners, race-walked the Bolder Boulder 25 times, and hiked the Inca Trail into Machu Picchu.

Calling Longmont, Colorado home, she continues to travel extensively.

www.CarolAnnWilson.com

How to Contact Carol Ann

Carol Ann Wilson
906 Cranberry Court
Longmont, Colorado 80503
720-600-5134
www.CarolAnnWilson.com
CarolAnn@CarolAnnWilson.com

Acknowledgments

With all of my various adventures and experiences, there are many who have supported me through all of it.

First of all is my family who have always been there for me.

Then, Barbara Stark and Ed Schilling were there to help me build my divorce training business.

Alan Gappinger is my close friend, advisor, and financial guru… I have never lost a cent with him, even in down markets.

Most of my books would not have happened without Judith Briles, my long term friend, advisor and editor.

My spiritual advisors, Marian and Glen Head, have always had time to listen to my woes, give advice and support.

And my 16 years with Sonny Stratton have been the happiest years of my life. There are so many others who have shared this eclectic life with me, it is impossible to list them all.

www.ingramcontent.com/pod-product-compliance
Lightning Source LLC
LaVergne TN
LVHW041936070526
838199LV00051BA/2807